GEORGE THOMAS OF SOHO

George Thomas

GEORGE THOMAS
OF
SOHO

D. FELICITAS CORRIGAN
of Stanbrook Abbey

SECKER & WARBURG · LONDON

First published in Great Britain 1970 by
Martin Secker & Warburg Limited
14 Carlisle Street, London W1V 6NN

© Stanbrook Abbey 1970

SBN 436 10880 1

Printed in Great Britain by
Western Printing Services Ltd, Bristol

For Mary
to whom George's life belongs
by every title of possession

Acknowledgements

During his lifetime George Thomas published three books: *A Tenement in Soho* (Jonathan Cape 1931), *My Mind a Kingdom* (Jonathan
Cape 1938), and *Neighbours* (Williams and
Norgate 1935). A fourth book entitled *To Dwell
with Happiness* failed to find a publisher. The
biographer wishes to express her thanks to
Messrs Jonathan Cape Ltd who gave ready
permission for the use of quotations from
the books published by them. The quotation
from T. S. Eliot on page 72 is reprinted by permission of Faber and Faber Ltd.

Contents

Contents

Preface by Sir Alec Guinness, C.B.E.

The triangle formed by the Catholic churches of Warwick Street to the west, Soho Square to the north and
Leicester Place to the south, encloses an area containing
the best delicatessen shops in England. It also encloses
some of the sleaziest vice to be found in London, a vast
amount of friendliness and good humour, a smattering
of street quarrels or sometimes brawls, and a large
slice of Cockney liveliness in Berwick Market. This
book tells of a noble life lived—at least in his formative
years—in the heart of this triangle by George Thomas.
He was born in 1903 and made a literary reputation for
himself with three books written while almost inert
through physical incapacity; but, in spite of the squalid
surroundings, he used his listening ear and observing
eye to such effect that he grew to wisdom and, finally,
to something approaching saintliness.

As a young actor I must have passed many times
under his window, or at least by the alleyway leading
to his room, as Berwick Market lies cheek by jowl with
some of London's most popular theatres; and yet I was
completely unaware of his existence. But I suppose
we do not have to be Levites just to pass by in ignor-
ance, averting our gaze, for most of us are merely

preoccupied with our own comings and goings, blind to what may be under our noses. Thomas is an eye-opener, and a disturbing yardstick with which to measure the trivia and essentials of life. He wrote, 'Always there is the spiritual inspiration of those who can remember that pain and suffering may be the heights and not the depths of life.' Here is a man who suffered and knew the heights. His story told by an enclosed Benedictine nun with imagination and humour is mercifully free from hagiology.

PART ONE
The Craft of Living

CHAPTER ONE · HARD TIMES

1903–1919

If there are names whose sound conveys sweet music to the ear, the name George Thomas is not one of them. All the same, there is a sturdy homespun quality about it that is not unattractive—it will obviously stand no nonsense. 'I'm not very fond of the saintly and royal George,' its owner was to admit, 'but I'd hate to have been Clarence or Montmorency.' The files of Somerset House must contain records of many a George Thomas, and a reader has the right to ask what claim this one in particular has upon his interest. A Cockney born and bred, he lived out his forty-nine years without having made any mark on society beyond the publication of two diaries which brought him very limited fame in England and the United States, and a novel which passed almost unnoticed. When he died in 1952, the world at large was not conscious of being any the poorer. Why then call attention to him now? Simply because as long as Englishmen draw breath, they will prize the valiant heart and man's unconquerable mind.

George Thomas, born on 23 February 1903, in Ganton Street in the West End of London, was the eldest son and the second of six children born to Alfred John Thomas, a staunch Protestant, and his equally staunch Catholic wife, Eleanor Ada Potter. The Thomases hailed from Helston in Cornwall, where they had been tailors for at least a hundred years until about 1870, when George's grandfather migrated to London with his Helston bride, and settled in Berwick Street, Soho. Here, in the unsalubrious Petticoat Lane of the West End, his descendants were to remain for sixty years.

When Eleanor Potter married Alfred Thomas in 1899, she did so because he was the only one of her suitors who positively liked work. By training he was a cook and waiter. The work was seasonal, and during the summer months he found employment as a porter in Covent Garden market. If either season overlapped, he was likely to find himself out of work for the next six months except for an occasional odd job. Until he obtained regular employment in 1914 under the Westminster City Council, he and his wife were frequently forced to lead a hand-to-mouth existence, driven to desperate extremities in order to remedy desperate need. It was during these lean years that Mrs Thomas gave birth to all but the youngest of her children: Ada in 1900, George in 1903, Albert in 1906, Daniel in 1910, and Arthur in 1913.

The children were no strangers to hunger. 'I remember often having to dip dry and very hard bread into tea for two good reasons,' George recalls. 'We had nothing to put on the bread, and it was too hard to be palatable. We used as children to get free soup and bread from a near-by hospice and, to preserve a shred of respectability, we had to make those scraps in a pillow-case look as much like "washing" as the knobbly crusts permitted.' To survive at all demanded all Mrs Thomas's skill and inventive genius. No woman could contrive a dinner better than she out of twopennyworth of butcher's scraps, a handful of lentils, and a few free bacon bones, but she could not mint money, and the rent had to be found somehow if they were to keep a roof over their heads. In 1910 their poverty reached its climax. Necessity knows no law, and if the law supposed that Eleanor Thomas would allow her children to be thrown on the street without bite or sup or shelter, then the law must be defied. At a lightning signal from their chief, the whole family struck camp:

Dad had been out of work for months and things were looking hopeless. Suddenly a street bookmaker came on the scene and Mother had an idea. Now a bookie must have a bolt-hole to get away from nasty troublesome police, and in this bookie's bolt-hole there happened to be rooms to let on the ground floor, so Mum moved into them. The rent was seven shillings per week; the racing gentleman paid 1/6d. per day for the privilege of hurriedly closing the door. Result for a full week: 2/- profit for Mum out of the arrangement. Mother and I are of the opinion that that period holds the clue to our complete physical breakdown. I was seven years of age, mercifully too young to understand. Dad eventually got work and I saw his wages—a sovereign. I danced and shouted, 'Hooray, Mum's ship has come home!'

The rooms into which they moved were on the ground floor of No. 4 Tyler's Court which runs between No. 6 and No. 7 Berwick Street. Here they spent fourteen months before returning to Berwick Street, and here Mrs Thomas gave birth to her third son, Dan. George has left a description of the place under the designation of Crow Court in his novel, *Neighbours*:

> Crow Court is one of those places that surprise the unsuspecting traveller along broader and better-known thoroughfares. In a few steps one has found and lost again a scene which the romantic call real London. One generally takes a step backwards for a more leisurely view under the dark tunnelled opening which leads to the three or four houses inside the court. The shadows disperse in the light that comes over the low shed-like building on one side, but reappear in the black exit at the farther end. The ground floor inhabitants have a blank wall facing their windows along the narrow court. The uneven paving and irregular doorsteps all denote age; it is real old London, decrepit with the cares of many generations.

Why, one asks, should hard-working, intelligent people tolerate life in such a quarter and under such conditions? The seven shillings' rent paid for two rooms in Tyler's Court (those in Berwick Street cost considerably more) represents roughly what must have been a third of many a working-man's weekly wage in the first decade of the present century. Millions were paying less for houses which, however mean, at least afforded privacy and even modest comfort. At this point the mind possibly recoils from the vision of deadening miles upon miles of grimy little dwellings, and turns in relief to Soho with its gesticulating cosmopolitan crowds, its narrow streets thick with exotic odours, its literary associations and relics of bygone opulence. Bygone indeed, for as today's police records testify, the once-fashionable town houses have degenerated into rack-rented tenements, the coffee houses and taverns into shady night clubs. Why then choose such dubious surroundings? In his novel *Neighbours* George Thomas offers an explanation:

> People lived in such places because of a paradox that was part of life itself; they could not rise higher, however hard they strove, and could not sink lower in a material sense. People in their proper senses did not come from the green countryside, did not leave the gardens and the flowers, fields and birds, to come and live in Crow Court. You did not choose to live here, you stayed where you were poked; and kids were brought into the world in places like the Court, because the people did not know any difference or did not care; but you did not go telling them tales about the bees and honey, the seaside and fresh air and sunshine. People in their proper senses did none of these things. And you did not tell the kids all they had to go through, but you saw that they grew used to it by teaching them to laugh at everything that went wrong.

In that last sentence George has summed up the policy of his own mother, for if ever woman taught her children by example the laughter that is sanity and sanctity combined, that woman was Eleanor Thomas. At first their laughter was that of healthy innocent childhood. The two elder children attended St Edward's, Dufours Place, a small school then attached to the Church of our Lady of the Assumption, Warwick Street. 'I think that going to school does not necessarily teach a child anything,' George once wrote to a friend. 'What I learned at school has stood me in good stead—not the lessons, elementary though they were, but qualities absorbed in the process of learning have given my mind a sure foundation, a faith in simple natural goodness.'

Religious instruction both morning and afternoon held pride of place in the daily time-table. The children were uniformly drilled in the 'Penny Catechism' learned by heart, and imbibed stories from the Scriptures or Lives of the Saints designed to inspire devotion and imitation. George was an apt pupil. Heaven was as real to him as earth. He loved to rise early and run along the almost deserted streets to Mass. The day went all the better for it.

With the exception of the thirteenth-century St Etheldreda's, Ely Place, George's parish church, St Mary's, Warwick Street, is the oldest and one of the most interesting Catholic churches in London. It has history and atmosphere. Once past the modern glass swing doors, you are transported to the eighteenth century, to the era of the Vicars-Apostolic and the Chapels-Royal of the foreign embassies. Its registers go back to 1735, although the actual foundation may date from the Stuarts. In the nineteenth century, Italian operatic singers made the church one of the most visited musical centres in the City. Perhaps something of its former glory still lingers about the place, for the choir there was one of the keen joys of George Thomas's boyhood. He had a passion for singing, and to his choir-training at St Mary's he owed that knowledge of the Mass and of the Latin language which was to add such a treasure to his mental resources in the years ahead.

His parish church held another and a supreme attraction. This was the large statue of the Blessed Virgin, neither ancient nor beautiful, which has become a well-known centre of devotion in London. It became stamped ineradicably upon his mind, and was interwoven with all his religious memories. 'There is a marvellous Lady Altar at Warwick Street, thousands of votive hearts in silver, cased all round,' he told a correspondent thirty years later. Then, realizing that the eye of youth had probably magnified their number, he added a modifying, 'anyway, it looks like thousands'. Rapt in wonder, the little fellow would stare fascinated at the coruscations of light from the innumerable candles and lamps. He longed to strike a sudden pretty blaze and see his own little pillar of fire refracted and reflected a thousand times over in that silver setting. But even the smallest candle cost a penny and he never had a penny to squander.

He grew up outwardly sturdy, possessed of the necessary moral as well as physical courage to deal a knock-out blow to a young ruffian determined to bully an inefficient teacher, but at the same time he was a silent

9

child who quietly looked on at the life around him, and drew from it conclusions kept for the most part to himself. In *A Tenement in Soho* he tells of one old woman who attracted him with her grey hair and troubled eyes. 'Each Thursday I would come across her near the school, always carrying a basket of washing. I could not carry it myself, but I took a handle.' By taking a handle he relieved her load and steadied his own legs, for as he approached his eleventh year, they were becoming very unsteady indeed. He had reached the age when intelligent boys look forward to College. He had plenty of ambition. He wanted to be a lawyer. All about him he saw poor people evicted for non-payment of rent. He made a habit of memorizing all the legal queries and replies in the weekly papers picked up from the market-dealers, and he was soon an expert in the complexities of the Rent Restriction Act. Like a Daniel among the Elders, the poor trusted his judgement and sought his advice. 'Ask George,' they would say in their difficulties; or, 'Go to George, he'll remember.' The nickname 'Lawyer Thomas' was to cling to him all his life, but he was never given the chance to study law. The doctors had already sealed his doom.

As early as 1910 when George was only seven, his sister's extreme debility had begun to puzzle one physician after another, until a Harley Street specialist finally diagnosed facio-scapulo-humeral myopathy. The medical label conveyed little to Mrs Thomas, although her own brother had been its victim for over twenty years. The condition—commonly known as muscular dystrophy—was to be traced to Mrs Thomas's mother, who had unknowingly transmitted to her son and daughter the disease which was to blight the lives of her grandchildren. What amounted in her to nothing worse than a weakness of the shoulder-girdle would render five of her descendants completely helpless. Ada was already stricken. Now it was George's turn.* His parents made the discovery:

> One evening my father and mother, who were seated each side of our wide fireplace, called me to them as I played in the room. They told me to lie flat on my back on the hearthrug and, without using my elbows, to sit up. I tried several times and could not do it. I rolled up on my elbow just in time to intercept a strange glance that passed between my parents. They said nothing of my inability to rise, but at that moment their fears for me were confirmed.

The school doctor arrived to make his routine inspection of the children and, after examining George, said something about 'six months' in the hearing of another child.

> This boy hastened to tell me, in horrified excitement, that I had six months to live. I did not believe him, and rejected the possibility with scorn. But that afternoon after school as I walked home, I

* Muscular dystrophy is a disease affecting primarily the skeletal muscles, the fibres of which undergo a degeneration which alters their structure and interferes with their function, so that there is weakness and finally paralysis of the muscles affected, accompanied by a progressive atrophy or wasting away of their substance.

glanced down the sunlit street and something hal-
ted me. Life was a wonderful adventure then. The
freshness of new discoveries and the joy of freedom,
playing in the streets or more rarely in the park,
constituted my whole existence for the moment.
I sat down on the edge of the kerb and knew a dark
despair. I wondered what would happen to the sunshine, and I felt my doom upon me like black night.
After a few minutes I rose up and went home to my
tea, and as the days passed, spent in school and play
and healthy sleep, I thought less and less about the
remark.

Within six months death did visit the family to claim,
not George, but the two-year-old Arthur whom he
had taken to the neighbouring park but a few days
before. Meanwhile George's father read the portents
of the future with heavy foreboding. He decided that
at all costs he must secure permanent employment. In
1914 therefore he entered the service of the Westminster
City Council where he remained, save for three years
spent in the army during the First World War, until his
retirement in June 1946.

Faced with disabled children [George relates], my
father showed considerable courage and good sense.
He decided on two things: to leave us to ourselves
as much as possible, and to attempt some kind of
security for us while he lived. He became a dustman,
finding security in the lowest job possible. But he
had his dignity. He saw his job as less authoritative
than a policeman's, but not less useful. He never
again wore a stiff shirt or swore at studs, and his

hands were well calloused, but he was adequate in his corduroys as in all his ways of life. His dignity claimed respect, and he did not express pity or need it. He was so quiet of manner that few ever heard him enter the tenement we lived in, and in the neighbourhood many were unaware of him alto-gether.

The tragedy of the household deepened with every month. For some time the doctors had had their suspicions of Mrs Thomas. In 1913, she and Ada under-went a five-weeks' examination in hospital while George spent the time in a Poor Law Home, an ex-perience he never forgot. In 1916 Mrs Thomas gave birth to her youngest son, Alfred, and immediately showed signs of muscular dystrophy. The same year saw the death of her widowed mother, whose dying legacy was her helpless son. 'While we've got a loaf, he can share it!' was Mrs Thomas's comment as she took her pitiable brother into her own home. After some years he developed suicidal mania and had to be re-moved, but not before the small boy who shared the same room had seen and heard enough to haunt him for the rest of his days.

At school, George was simply marking time until the law released him and cast him loose upon the world. The frustration of these years of promise when he was hungry for knowledge and mental training was later to occasion a blistering castigation of the educational system of the time: 'A rotten, thoroughly rotten sys-tem, but what a loss to humanity! It is a *spiritual* stunt-ing. Mental development restricted, consequently warped and immature characters.' During his last years at school, his muscles grew appreciably weaker. At twelve he could still play cricket, at thirteen the game was beyond him. Falls became frequent and violent. Upon leaving school, a place was offered him in an office, but just then he developed pneumonia, went into hospital instead, and so forfeited the job. When he recovered, the only work available was a stall in the Berwick Street market. There he spent eighteen months. Then, as he was unable to stand erect or support himself any longer on his legs, his mother consented to send him to a Catholic institution in Yorkshire. There he passed with sudden and bitter transition from childhood to maturity:

After a long train journey [he writes], I got out at a tiny country station. I had to wait for a conveyance. The night was dark and rain fell heavily. On the open platform there was a bench and I sat there and waited. A pony cart came for me, and through the dead of night we drove on for a grotesque couple of miles. I had never before been in the country in the dark. No one spoke to me. We stopped near a wall. I saw a door. Slowly the door opened, and a hunchback came out carrying a lantern. Inside, the light swung about as the hunchback moved, and the first thing I noticed was a large locked collecting-box, and above it three words: HOME FOR INCURABLES.

I had arrived. Here I was to settle—into dust. Up to that moment I had not thought of myself as incurable. I had been the specimen at lectures for medical students, but until that instant I had not been presented so baldly with the truth and my last resting place. I was never more shocked. My father was in the army then, and my mother had been encouraged to let me go to a place in the country where I could learn a trade. The trade that a piece of old iron learns on its scrap-heap.

I arrived two days before Christmas. By June I had managed to convince those at home that the place was unsuitable, and the following six months were spent in attempts to get me away. I arrived home two days before Christmas. I had gone away a boy, but I returned a man.

CHAPTER TWO · TUITION FREE

He was two months short of sixteen. Cigarette in hand, the burly youth greeted his mother in a gruff voice with a broad Yorkshire accent. She eyed him from head to foot, and with a nod at the cigarette asked: 'And where are you going to get the money for those?' He considered her question for a moment, and then without a word he slowly put the glowing thing out. He never smoked again. He had come home, home to her astringent commonsense and his mother's love. He needed both. From now onwards he had to see life as a member of a family in which first one, then two, then three, and finally four had to discover means of preserving their human dignity against almost insuperable odds. Things bad could only get worse. There could be no alleviation.

Faced with the certain prospect of deep suffering of long duration, a man normally reacts in one of three ways. He may beat and break himself against the destiny to which he is chained, until in despair he puts a violent end to what he cannot undo; or, unresisting, he may allow the stream of life to bear him passively along until he becomes as supine in mind and will as he is nerveless and sinewless in body; or, strong in supernatural faith, he may enter into the simple but momentous truth that life is God's greatest gift, a man's condition God's appointment, and that it is wisdom to take it, use it, and improve it.

Without seeing the course ahead so clearly defined, George Thomas instinctively knew that he had to fight. Before following him into the arena, it may be well to take stock of his environment in order to see how far his untaught mind was equipped to meet the exigencies that might arise.

For thirty years of his life Berwick Street was George's university, his metropolis of knowledge, the occupants of the tenement in which he lived and the street-traders below his window were his tutors. In his diaries he has left a picture of this world which no one would have dared to invent. Now a diary is an historical document that cannot be gainsaid. 'Inspired verse, inspired doctrine, inspired morals come first'—thus does Hilaire Belloc graduate witnesses to truth—'but after these, diaries'. George's have been freely used throughout this book.

No. 6 Berwick Street, where for twenty years the Thomases rented three rooms on the second floor, was a partly-timbered old house four rooms deep behind a shop front. Between it and the neighbouring house, the builders had contrived a well or shaft in order to convey light and air to the middle rooms. Seven windows in the house looked into this well, one into Tyler's Court, the rest into Berwick Street. There was one sink in the house, and everyone drew their water from the one tap over it. All water had to be carried up, and all slops down. There was no yard, and wet washing was hung across the landing of the staircase to dry. The principal tenants scarcely altered throughout the years, however many guests came or went. A family of thrifty Italians, one of the five children mentally retarded, lived on the ground floor at street level; the first floor was occupied by Jews; in addition to the Thomases' three rooms on the next floor were two reached by back stairs from the landing, one given over to a bibulous Irishman named Murphy, the other to two wrangling women, Mrs Grey and Lizzie Batt, afflicted with the same long thirst; the top floor was the domain of Mr and Mrs Paddie and their two offspring. For many years these remained in residence until the local authorities condemned the house as being unsafe and gave them all notice to quit. Amid the general hubbub that resulted, George decided to amuse his mother and conserve the memory of events by jotting them down each day, and reading them aloud to the family in the evening. Nothing was studied, exaggerated or falsified. He sets the scene thus:

12 January. Young Paddie, the boy who lives upstairs, is twenty years old today, and quite early I had the opportunity of wishing him 'Many happy returns'. Later on I offered to retract my greetings. He had bought a few gramophone records and lent them to a friend. His father objected, and being a vicious character began to punch into his son. There was a terrific row, and I heard the boy say, 'If you

don't leave me alone, I'll hit you with a hammer!'
Suddenly he rushed downstairs, and a large and very
heavy glass cigarette stand followed him. Small
wonder he was in a hurry!

24 January. This evening listened to Mr Murphy
reacting in his cups to the shock of the 'notice' of
yesterday. We heard: 'Chuck me out of the 'ouse,
would they? . . . I'm an old soldier I am. . . . There's
me in khaki over there. . . . Got to respect the
British Army. . . . Never see us running away. . . .
Old soldiers never die. . . . I know what I'll do, I'll
burn the ruddy house down. . . .' He stumbled
across the room humming a tune, and in a final
burst of defiance began to play the gramophone. It
has had a broken spring for years, so that when
music is required, he has to stand over the instru-
ment winding all the time.

10 March. The family upstairs, having been relieved of their youngest child, Eileen, has today
experienced a further relief. The woman, on her
return from work, came in and said with a grin,
'Have you heard? Tom's got a month!' 'What for?'
I asked. 'Fighting; bashing a feller in a pub. . . .
Serve him right,' his loving spouse remarked, 'it
will teach him to leave people alone!'

16 March. Exodus, chapter one! A Chinese who
was a subtenant in the house has removed. A taxi
sufficed to transport him and his goods and chattels
elsewhere. It was the quaintest removal I have ever
heard of. Alfie helped the forlorn Oriental to carry
downstairs two suitcases, one chair, an oil stove and
frying pan, one jug, and—a basin of undried washing! He was not to depart so overloaded, however,

for suddenly the Chinaman with whom he shared rooms came down, grabbed the jug, and with the utmost composure trotted upstairs again. These Celestials understand the futility of words.

7 April. I am afraid that Alfie has had a bad time of it all round. His latest bother is an outburst of recrimination on the part of the old Hebrew woman. She put some fish in a jar on her window-sill with a saucer for covering, and thought it safe from interference. At the street door she met Alfie with a long pole by means of which he had 'dobbed up' some money from an area. Later the old woman found that the jar had been knocked over and the saucer broken, and then remembered Alfie and the pole. She lay in wait for him in a fine temper. Alfie protested in vain, and now we can hear her break out every few minutes with a, 'May they *all* be paralysed . . . because I am only a ruddy Jew they knock my fish over. . . . May they *all* be paralysed!'

Shut up within four walls, George stored up every scrap of experience. On a mind as impressionable as his, days and hours did the work of years. As time went on, he did not confine himself to the diary form, and his unpublished papers contain a few full-length portraits of the inmates and frequenters of his home. One or two he venerated, he tolerated most, and accepted all. Not unnaturally he saw in some of them counterparts of Dickensian characters, for Dickens and he sprang from the same soil and spoke the same language. The boy who ran a stall in Berwick Street market felt an instinctive affinity with the man who had spent his youth pasting labels on pots of blacking in a crazy old shack at the back of Hungerford Market while his father served a sentence in the Marshalsea. So he at once christened the gentle soul whose goodness sweetened his childhood memories, Captain Cuttle:

When my mother was weakening, he began to visit us regularly on washing day, and in his old age learned a little of the mysteries of a wash tub. He never mastered washing shirts, and Mother was for ever telling him to do the collar and cuffs properly. He would reply unfailingly, 'God bless my heart and soul, you will be doing this yourself next week', but he came for years. He had one little habit. He could not resist a piece of string if he saw it in the street, and he usually rolled it neatly and put it in his pocket. This custom—stonemason-like he used to tie his corduroys under the knee—landed him in a serious predicament. He was seen to pick up some string, and was arrested on suspicion of having committed a murder. A small boy had been found strangled with a piece of string. Unfortunately the family of the child was known to the old man. On learning of the crime, he cried piteously. He never touched a piece of string again.

Even the cats knew him by sight, although by then he was blind himself. He remembered them and always bought them meat. He had not seen any of them but he knew them by their table-manners, as the more adventurous would climb up his trouser-leg to get their heads into his coat pocket. He was often a pathetically lovely sight as he stood surrounded by cats, afraid to move for fear of treading on his friends. He would stand there helpless until someone came to rescue him, and all he ever said was, 'Lord bless my heart and soul', over and over again. I believe he was one of the truly blessed, and counted among the meek.

Whereas Captain Cuttle commanded George's affections, it was the Hogarthian figure of Mary Ann Carey who commanded his closest attention. Years afterwards, he was to make her the central character of his novel *Neighbours*. The fictional Mary Ann, however, is a piece of idealized hagiography; in real life, she was an incorrigible rogue:

Mary Ann knew only the expediencies of extreme want: a shelter, food, and the occasional luxury of a drop of rum. She would steal anywhere. In empty rooms she would take the door-handles for old iron, and would pick up bits of string in the streets. It all added up into pence. She received parish relief and was only allowed cash in kind from a provision stores. She would buy tea and sugar which she re-sold at shop price to her friends. She visited an old blind woman in the back part of my tenement in Soho, who lived on a blind pension and a few shillings from lodgers in her spare room. Mary Ann sold her a pound of sugar and a quarter of tea. She was given shop price. As she left, she thoughtfully took back the tea.

On her way downstairs she stole some newly-washed linen from a line on the landing, belonging to the old Jewess. It was the last time she entered the house unwatched. Whenever she came up to see Mother—which was like being faced with forty-five years of unblinking history of herself—a chair was

22

placed for her by the wall opposite the table, as far away from the knives, forks and spoons as she could be put. Mother knew, without asking, the desperate need that brought her, and she usually served a meal. The last visit I recall was when she came to ask if Mother would allow me to write out a faked rent-book showing the rent regularly paid, so that she could get a new lodging. Mother declined.

When over eighty years old Mary Ann fell down a flight of stairs and broke an arm, but it mended easily. She was eighty-four when she died, the old battler. She had not always been predatory; circumstances, courage and her sharp wits made her like that. The seasonal decline in the tailoring trade defeated her, but how she survived to that age baffles me.

For years Mary Ann's blind victim had shared a tiny back room amid noisy strife with her morose companion, Mrs Grey. When at last Liz had to be forcibly removed to an institution, she left her rival in possession of unwonted and unwanted peace. For 'Old Misery', to give Mrs Grey her popular title, was constitutionally incapable of enjoying anything, and the absence of Liz's brazen throat merely added one more wrong to her grievances. She existed on a disablement pension of eight shillings a week, to which her lodger Mr Murphy added his contribution of £1. Out of this sum she paid 11/4d. weekly for her two back rooms on the second floor, and the two of them lived on what was left. At any moment of day or night, without so much as a preparatory knock, she would make her entry into the Thomases' home to air her indignation, help herself to an onion, or borrow a novel. Offered a choice between Ben Hur and an Edgar Wallace, she unhesitatingly chose the detective story because, 'I don't feel in the mood to read about Jesus—God rest His soul!' Indeed she found all religion cold and comfortless. What was the use of it when it could not so much as relieve an attack of acute indigestion? 'Nothing don't seem to do it no good. I've been to Mass too and that ain't done it no good neither. You can't kid me there's anything in that stuff; I say there's nothing, when you're dead, you're dead, I say.' George studied her as a scientist might an entomological specimen. With the cruelly-clear sight of the young, he noted the twitching hands, the abnormally bright eyes, the pallid face, the leaden voice. She showed him the dun prison-house the years might bring, but her very apathy and dejection braced and nerved him, and made him hold up his head. A life such as hers without animation, spring or nobility must never become his.

At the opposite pole from Old Misery was the man under whose tutelage George Thomas derived many of the guiding principles of his early life. Tom Paddie, the jail-bird, lacked neither courage nor a saving sense of humour, and twenty years' imprisonment off and on for his manifold indiscretions must surely have earned him in the court of final judgement a sentence of 'condemnation into everlasting redemption'. He has already made his presence felt when he sent the glass weapon hurtling after his erring son. He makes his formal entry upon arrival home after an enforced rest:

> The man upstairs returned today after his month away from home. He has a grievance and has been sadly disillusioned. 'It ain't like it used to be. . . . No, it's *much* different! They've got new rules now, and they teach yer a trade. I didn't like it. It's orl right for the young 'uns, but I prefer the old rules.' This we heard as he talked with Mr Murphy, the old drunk downstairs; we also learned: 'They lets yer have a shave with a safety razor now, that's better than it used to be.' And with much puffing and blowing he washed himself at the sink on the landing, as if he was finally ridding himself, by means of his ablutions, of all the unpleasantness.

A heavily-built man of enormous strength, Tom Paddie was an honest man ready to accept work and give of his best, but he was unskilled and unwanted. When George wrote of him in *A Tenement in Soho* he had spent over ten years in almost continuous unemployment. He lumbered from home to market, from market to public house in search of something to do, and not finding it worked off his ebullient spirits in a war of words which often led to blows and landed him in the police court. His frequent holidays as His Majesty's guest had provided him with a store of adventures which he drew upon freely for George's benefit; there was nothing he enjoyed so much as an appreciative listener. And George was appreciative. He had a positive affection and a lively fellow-feeling for the older man, and endured his garrulity in order to sit in silence while he mentally analysed and compared their respective lots. The tales became parables, each with an inner meaning symbolical of something fine in the spirit of man:

He showed me that there are more precious things than physical freedom. In his early life he had been a foolish dupe for criminals, and he paid for the misdeeds of others, but he never lost his self-respect, and never allowed an affront to his conception of his own dignity as a man to go unpunished. On one occasion a police-sergeant and he came to blows; as a result of the effectiveness of his protest he was sentenced to eighteen months with hard labour. The first person he met on his release from prison was the sergeant, who was not waiting outside the gates by accident. 'See what you get for interfering with me?' he asked. Nothing more was said as nothing more was necessary. The man 'protested' again—and went back with another sentence. Wherever he went, he was free.

My jail-bird had his ideas about punishment. It was false to suppose that punishment automatically followed the isolation of the body; it worked in most cases because we fear all but voluntary enclosure. He said he did not realize this himself until he got the idea from a book while in prison. So far as society is concerned, imprisonment is as effective as legal murder, but death became the chief weapon employed at one time in the social war against ideas. This too was a fallacy, because ideas were imperishable and could not be eliminated by the removal of the thinker, especially if the thinker was a talker as well. The State assumed the right of capital punishment because dangers to the State arose from ideas. When I asked him what book gave him these ideas, he replied that it was about an old chap in Greece, who had to drink poison as a punishment because he talked too much. I still remember the Falstaffian roar of laughter which accompanied his answer. But here was my jail-bird hinting at a form of immunity through mental discipline and self-mastery.

Like Tom Paddie, George too must make himself immune, must somehow detach his mind from his surroundings so as to free himself from the spiritually destructive effects of his environment in his helpless bodily state. As he sat listening night after night, he slowly saw that life itself was God's greatest gift to man, and that on those terms he was equal to all his fellow-men. 'Of talents all I can say is that we each have one, and that is to transmute experience, to take the raw material of life and put the imprint of the human creature upon it, so that when we are aware of conscious living as we are aware of our thoughts and the sights and sounds of life, we shall know we have transformed mere existence into joy, peace, beauty and love. We have to put the carat stamp of quality on life, or all other talents avail us nothing.'

Had George Thomas's experience been limited to the single level of society to be found in the tenement, time might have proved him ill-equipped to meet the future. He might have come to regard his neighbours with a half-affectionate derision, or else found refuge

27

in a dream-world of his own contriving. But a powerful influence has yet to be considered, namely, the Berwick Street market. With its colour, its crowds and its cries, it was woven into the very texture of his life from 1907 to 1930. 'It is a never-failing lure,' he writes, 'and has held us all with its ever-changing attractiveness for nearly twenty years.' In its early days before the First World War, the market was little more than a motley collection of barrows and stalls, offering cheap fruit and vegetables to housewives out for a bargain. These days of Utopian free trade came to an end when Jewish merchants approached the street-vendors with offers to rent the stalls for two shillings a night. At a single stroke they wrought a transformation. Out of their travelling cases they drew bales of silk and cloth, cosmetics, leather goods and furs. Not to be outdone, the butchers, fishmongers and fruiterers already established in adjacent shops set up their own booths in the open air. Brisk competition sent the price of stalls soaring, improved the quality of the goods, and created a scene of picturesque *chiaroscuro* in the heart of fashionable London. Rents soon rose to £3 a week, and so bitter was the rivalry that the authorities finally stepped in and demanded that all vendors hold a trader's licence.

The market was in its heyday when George Thomas undertook the management of a stall after leaving school. Here the would-be lawyer had to turn pedlar and drive a trade in matches, tape, soap and such small wares as were easily portable and easily procurable. From his house to the stall was but one step, he took that step for almost eighteen months, and that was as far as he ever stepped into the world of everyday life. Nevertheless it was a strangely cosmopolitan world in which he found himself. The many-hued crew—Indians, Greeks, Chinese, Italians, French, Germans—made the boy, who had never been farther afield than the nearest park, travel-conscious. They introduced him to most of the holes and corners of Europe and the East, and in doing so, broadened and softened his sympathies. George has delineated one of them in some detail:

One man, an Albanian, who spoke eight languages fluently and was a fine violinist, had six unmarried sisters and their parents were dead. A keen business man, he yet had a contempt for money which puzzled me until I discovered how he disposed of his profits. Although a street-trader, he bought from Czecho-Slovakia in considerable quantities and his business was very lucrative. He saved carefully, and after some years he had provided his sisters with the dowries necessary in their country, and had married them all off. Not until then, a man of middle age with hair greying at the temples, did he settle his own affairs. He went away one summer leaving a friend in charge of his stall, and returned in the late autumn with his own wife, a bride of three weeks, from Egypt. She was a strikingly beautiful woman. I heard of his return at the same time as I heard of the tragedy of his homecoming. She died of pneumonia almost at once. Soon after this the street-market ceased to be profitable and he disappeared.

In his essay *My Mind to Me*, Walter de la Mare has reviewed various modes of travel: into foreign parts, into the past, the present, the future, the mountains of the moon, or into the heart and mind of man. Whereas, he observes, the practised traveller often brings back astonishingly little, 'a twilight expedition even to the nearest pillarbox may present another order of traveller with an evening star that seems in its serene and solitary beauty to have been awaiting the assignation until that very moment. It is not distance that counts, or hope, or even longing; but the mind's looking-glass, which not only reflects but transmutes all that it receives.' George Thomas was incapable of a journey even to the nearest pillarbox. But when at sixteen years of age his journeying through physical space was done, the knapsack of his mind was already packed with the most valuable of all human treasures —ideas. Life was to afford him plenty of leisure in which to sort and project them on their travels into the space where his thoughts would have free range.

CHAPTER THREE · ALL
THE YEAR ROUND

1920–1927

February 23, 1919, his sixteenth birthday, was the milestone from which George was to measure the years spent indoors. 'I well remember that morning when, putting one foot downstairs, I knew what would happen if I persisted.' Arthur being dead, the family now consisted of father, mother, daughter and four sons. Mrs Thomas had rarely ventured out of doors since the birth of her youngest in 1916. By the year 1919 she was practically immobile. In the same year Ada, a frail attractive girl with a wealth of lovely hair, had to give up her flower-making with the French Wreath Company, although by sheer will-power she would cling to independence for another twelve years before surrendering to a life on wheels. George was less fortunate. From its first onset, the disease attacked him more grievously than the others. No one ever knew his height for he was unable even with support to stand upright; he had to be lifted from bed to chair and from chair to bed. Two of his brothers, Albert and Alfred, were to remain free from the family trouble. The third, born in 1910, the irresistible and irrepressible Dan or 'Ginger' as he was called from his mop of red hair, was still a child at school under close medical observation. In a very short time he too would succumb, and as 'one of us' would complete the spirited quartet cooped up within the three rooms on the second floor of No. 6 Berwick Street.

The most important room of the three, family kitchen by day, mother's bedroom by night, measured exactly ten feet square and never saw the sun:

> A few days ago, Mother, in talking with Mrs Grey, made a remark which went almost unnoticed. They were talking about the fine weather we have had lately and the neighbour said, 'It is a lovely day *outside*; the sun is quite bright!' Mother replied, unconscious of the infinite pathos in her statement, 'Yes, I know, I can see its reflection on the white building opposite.'

But Mrs Thomas was not the woman to waste time on self-pity. Her kitchen was her court and she reigned over it like a queen. Not that she was a dominating matriarch. Before strangers she was diffident and nervous to excess, but with her own it was different. Her speech was simple and downright, but none knew better than her children that even if reinforced by a stick of high explosives, it masked a penetration and tenderness which had no thought but for their welfare. It was well for them that she was 'the captain of the crew'.

Mr Thomas deferred in everything to his wife. 'You've got brains what I ain't got,' he told her, 'and you know how to manage the money when you get it.' And he saw to it that she did get it. As soon as he was de-mobilized in 1919, he resumed work as a dustman under the Westminster City Council. Each week he put into her hand never a penny less than £2 10s. 0d., and with the remaining 18/– he paid for his breakfasts, boots, beer and tobacco. A dustman's wage did not mean affluence exactly, but it was sufficient to steer clear of the Skilly of the moneylender and the Char Bydis of the workhouse, as Alfred Doolittle would have said. Not that Alfred Thomas and Alfred Doolittle were birds of a feather. Bernard Shaw's stage dustman, born of a Welsh mother and brought up in Hounslow, and the dustman of real life, born of a Cornish mother and brought up in Soho, have little in common beyond their Christian names, their costume, and their dust-manship. For however gaily Eliza Doolittle's father might blossom out into frock-coat, silk hat, shares in the Pre-digested Cheese Trust, and King's English, George Thomas's would content himself all his days with his old corduroys, his felt hat with its back brim covering neck and shoulders, his weekly pittance, and his proper tongue. He had one aim in life, and only one —to give his crippled family a feeling of security. While he had two hands able to work, they should not want. For thirty years on end, he was to turn night into day. 'We dine late,' George writes, 'not because it is "the thing" in the best circles, but because Dad is a night-worker, and that mode is the most convenient for all.' With a wry smile over the counter-attraction of The Newcastle-upon-Tyne, he adds: 'Dad's vocation is that of being a potman, but his duty is that of being a

33

dustman.' Often enough the father managed to combine both duty and vocation. After a night's heavy work he would call on a friendly publican with offers of help in exchange for a few books, a bundle of clothing, or a pot of stew—to say nothing of the glass of free beer—and then trudge home to light a fire, roll out pastry, wash dishes and scrub a floor, or clumsily attend to the needs of his wife and children before taking sanctuary in the bed vacated by his two healthy sons, who by that time were about their daily work. 'Dad comes home and the place is obviously cold and miserable,' George notes in December, 'and yet as often as not, even after getting wet through working all night, he sets to and lights us a fire; alternatively, he occasionally says a few "blasts" and tells Dan to light the fire.'

It is possible, as Chesterton has observed, to look at a thing nine hundred and ninety-nine times with perfect safety, but to look at it for the thousandth time is to be in frightful danger of seeing it for the first time. Superficially father and eldest son were unlike in everything except outward appearance, for the children who had inherited their mother's disease resembled their father in colouring and features, the sons who escaped resembled their mother. George found conversation with his father difficult; he could only talk to him about 'odds and ends of things'. Much as he respected and loved him, he did not perhaps look at him with a seeing eye until after his mother's death, and only then did he discern in him the very embodiment of his own ideals. Mr Thomas moves in and out of his son's diaries as he moved in and out of his own home, with quiet unconcern, solitary and independent, a Protestant in a Catholic household, a stout Conservative in a Labour stronghold, inarticulate, bewildered and stolid amid a circle of eager reflective minds and eloquent tongues. And yet Dad diffuses his own radiance. He lives in the memory like the figure of some massive peasant hewn in oak by Ernst Barlach, wide-brimmed felt hat pressed close about the patient face, sturdy form wrapped in the rhythmical folds of an ash-covered smock, plodding through the night with dutiful dogged foot in the teeth of driving sleet and storm. And as the image fades into the distance, the battered brim of the old hat seems on a sudden to twist and coil and wreathe itself into a triumphant volute surrounding his head with a nimbus of glory.

Hero or saint, in his own eyes he was only doing his job and he never thought twice about it. He was taken for granted. It was the mother who was the heart and soul of the family. The love between mother and children created that strong bond of unity which must strike any reader of George Thomas's diaries. These reveal with what zest she entered into all their interests, their discussions, and when necessary, their silences. Little escaped her. Her eye was quick to detect their present sufferings, and her wise counsel sought to forewarn and forearm them against those of the future. She saw clearly enough the anguish that lay before her sensitive eldest son, and she did what she could to harden and temper his spirit. She solemnly warned him that if anyone ever showed interest in him,

35

he must remember that it sprang from pity, or from devotion to social welfare work:

I saw a good deal of soundness in this advice, and it did not occur to me to question its wisdom. Do not expect the warmth of real understanding, or the joy and beauty of love. There would be sympathy, pity, kindness and condescension, but otherwise I was to consider myself dehumanized. It was a warning that increased sensibility involved increased susceptibility; but as I had already seen what the institutional scrap-heap does to the mind and spirit, the way ahead was obvious to me. The stark reality of life could only be painful, the rest depended on myself alone. Literally by the grace of God, I saw that the main values life had for me must be found within myself. The inner realities were the supports.

The mother who thus equipped him to face his lot taught him first by her own example. To her sober matter-of-factness in human affairs she united an almost tangible awareness of God's presence, of His almighty sustaining power, His incomprehensible ways, His inescapable will. This endowed her with that clearsightedness, fearlessness and wisdom which are the hallmark of those who live by supernatural faith. 'I can tell you quite seriously,' George assured a friend, 'that we three and Mother believe in a special Providence for ourselves. The worse we get the better things have become in certain respects. Mother wrote in my autograph book an apparently cynical remark which to us has its own special humour of faith; real faith has a sense of fun and mischief. She wrote, "God helps those who can't help themselves." Without the underlining, that is entirely cynical in an autograph book.'

Mrs Thomas was not yet forty when she found herself pent up for the rest of her life within the four walls of her kitchen. But the walls were not hung with dreams. Having already watched one of the family end in lunacy, she and her children resolved to lead as natural a life as possible, disregard their invalid state, and shun day-dreaming. To counterbalance the common life forced upon them, they made up their minds to respect independence of spirit and ignore one another. Where room space allowed, they would lead separate lives. To co-ordinate their efforts, they adopted three mottoes. To Romans 8.28, 'To them that love God, all things work together unto good', they added the companion axiom, 'Everything has a purpose', and crowned both with characteristic humour and catholicity of taste by the Confucian maxim, 'Our greatest glory is not in never falling, but in rising every time we fall.' Scarcely a day passed on which they did not put Confucius to the test, for Ada and Dan were subject to frequent falls:

> Mrs Levy, the old Hebrew woman below, once said to us, 'When I hear a bump I think, what is that? And I say, One of them has fallen down, but the bump breaks my gas-mantle just the same!'

Since George never walked, he at least could not miss his footing, but sitting down was no synonym for comfort. When not in bed, his only comparatively restful position was to sit up to the table in the airy front room away from the distressing heat and odours of the kitchen. Here he would remain most of the day, dragging himself into the kitchen when necessary on 'George's legs', an ordinary wooden chair with its back sawn off. In *A Tenement in Soho* we catch a glimpse of the boy on these heroic journeyings. It was Sunday evening. Sitting in the front room solitary and dejected, he opened St John's Gospel, read a passage meditatively, and found in it the strength he sought. Considerably more cheerful, he tells us, 'I went back into the kitchen to announce my intention of retiring. Mother asked, "Don't you want any supper?" "No thanks," I replied. "Have you come back only to tell us you are going to bed?" Mum queried. "Yes," I answered, "Goodnight." And Mum continued: "Well, all I can say is, you've some pluck to keep on struggling round on that chair!" and with a grin we exchanged final "Goodnights".' His mother knew him too well to remonstrate. During his early years indoors he often chose to go hungry: 'Hunger became part of my anguish. I refused food and went to bed miserable. My mother left me to myself, knowing that a healthy appetite could be used most helpfully in reverse. Sure enough by the next morning nature had restored the normal balance of body and mind.' Quite apart from the contempt of food which sprang from his choking misery, the very conditions of his life imposed a daily fast which to most people would be insupportable. Meals were a matter of luck: 'On Monday we generally have a cup of tea and some buttered bread about twelve o'clock; then, after Nurse has been we have more tea and bread, and get our dinner about nine o'clock at night.'

The asceticism of the most austere religious Order becomes child's play compared with the poverty and abstinence which the Thomases accepted with such cheerful unconcern, yet there were times when the bleak reality of such a life brought George to the brink of despair: 'Years of this attenuated existence, and then total oblivion. I nearly wrote, Thank God! But there is no God at such times; at least, not until the morrow.'

Far keener than any physical pain was his sense of frustration and his dependence upon others for the slightest service. Letters to friends written on Tuesday might be posted after much pleading on Friday night or even not at all. 'I ought to get into a bad temper over it but somehow I can't,' he writes. 'All I can think is, "They don't understand. . . . They don't understand".' Yet that spirit of his was in training, and in his secret heart he knew it:

Take a man, chain him to a wall, restrict his movements by further chains, and one has an analogy which illustrates to some extent my handicap. It is true in a double sense, physically and mentally. Yet I know that when the physical chains are forged complete, my mind will still chafe at the restriction, but as it leaps, to be pulled up with a jolt, I see the lesson that is to be learned from it and could smile at the thought which would suggest loss to me—I have *gained* something—but it is difficult to be patient.

Here it would be pleasant to record that the Catholic faith, implanted at birth and nurtured in home and school, carried George Thomas triumphantly over every obstacle. As it was, his faith was seemingly the first thing to go:

At school religion was as real to me as the multiplication tables. God was the Creator of all things. Jesus was His Son born of the Virgin Mary. His Church was infallible in teaching faith or morals. Many things were sinful, from wasting time that belonged to your employer, to coveting your neighbour's wife, whatever that might mean. The day I discovered that in some quarters religion was held to be nothing more than a superstition was an astonishing day for me. It was the flat contradiction of religious teachings in everyday life that gave me my first insight into adult behaviour. Total contradiction, not just isolated examples. In the grown-up world nearly all the sins and most of the vices were well-favoured.

The tension between the world of sense and the intangible world of the supernatural became overpowering. They seemed to have no common meeting-ground, no point of contact:

To readjust my world, I had to endure the impact of worldliness on those thoughts and impressions that were the inner life of my mind. Along with religious teaching, I had absorbed legends without being aware that they were legends. These became most unreal when in daily life I found the practice of religion left to a few. The truth of religion, the imperative need to worship and give thanks, and the practical spiritual guidance it gave for personal happiness, appeared to be things of the distant past. Added to this confusion was the pain and stress of being locked out from a full social and emotional life because of my increasing disablement.

By slow degrees, he began to regard faith as a clouding-over of the intellect. To submit to authority meant to lose one's independence, to fetter one's mind and lock oneself in a pen set about with moral shibboleths and ecclesiastical taboos. His body might be imprisoned but his mind was free, and he was not going to let the priests put his eyes out. Seeing was believing, as another Thomas had said before him. His own intellect must search, sift, scrutinize and test before he would admit anything to be true. Reason rose in revolt: 'I was thrown back upon myself completely. I rejected all authority as a binding, limiting influence. Only privately was I unable to throw off my religious views, but I took care to paraphrase my thoughts, so that they were ambiguous in a pagan way.'

In following George Thomas's difficulties, one simple if homely fact must not be overlooked: his surname was Thomas, and to doubt was in a sense a family game. 'I was really only being a doubting Thomas,' he writes in a youthful letter. 'If I were a Doctor of Philosophy I should make my first rule this: Question everything. That is a jolly good start.' So when left to his own resources, the first thing this disciple of the doubting Apostle did was to turn a critical eye upon his own beliefs and set out to explore the heroic domain of unbelief.

Outwardly life went on as usual. The boy made no attempt to enlarge upon his ideas to those at home, or to cut himself off from the Sacraments. Apart from the formal occasions when the parish priest brought the invalids Holy Communion, they rarely saw him. But if the priest found it beyond his powers to thread his way through the labyrinth of tenements, not so the Scotswoman from Perth, 'our lovely Sister Anthony', as George with unwonted enthusiasm calls her. In her grey-blue habit and stiff white-winged cornette, she moves with ease and grace among the courts and alleys. We meet her in George's diaries bringing blessed ashes to the imprisoned family to remind them it is Ash Wednesday, beautifying their room with jonquils, daffodils and camellias for their Easter Communion, providing George with a Bible for study and a stout oak chair, and Mum with a statue of St Anthony of Padua, patron of the poor. Soho was her natural habitat. Mary Ann, Mrs Grey, the old drunk, the jail-bird, sheep clad in white, black, spotted or speckled fleeces, they were her children and she loved them every one. 'Nothing came amiss to her,' George writes, 'from nursing the sick poor, to shopping, and even to the scrubbing of floors. Some days she would come to us in the early afternoon and sit down happily for a talk. In a minute or two she would nod her head and doze, then start up guiltily and carry on the conversation where we had left off. When I think of such as Mary Ann, I also think of saintly Sister Anthony, and understand more than was ever made clear in a hundred sermons.' The nun's weekly visits were a spiritual oasis in George's life, and unconsciously she did much to preserve his spiritual balance simply by being what she was.

Lacking all guidance or counsel, he now began to read voraciously. As usual he found himself at the mercy of his environment. Being unable to go to a library, he had to accept whatever his often illiterate borrower selected. Novels were the obvious choice, and from Ethel M. Dell and Robert Hitchens he worked steadily through Dickens and Trollope to Tolstoy, Turgeniev, Dostoievsky and Chekov. 'I found the Russians more significant,' he declares. 'The darker the horror of the tenement descriptions the nearer they were to my blackest feelings. I could sympathize with the hopelessness, for the descriptions were an outward symbol of the darkness of the psychological night portrayed.' It was Chekov who threw him a raft which kept him afloat for some years:

> In a short story by Chekov I came across a phrase that absorbed me. The story was *The Bishop* and I have forgotten it, but the phrase was, 'Everything is relative, approximate or conditional.' I knew that great authors were men of general culture and special insight, and this added to its effect. It kept my mind poised and open, told me how to look at and how to judge whatever happened to me. The starting point of my own reasoning was that we were released from the prison of the womb into the prison-house of the mind, and that from the

moment of birth we were all sentenced to solitary confinement for the rest of our time on earth. The Chekov phrase fitted this very well, and I could still relate all other things to God and His purpose.

Meanwhile his mind was mercifully to be deflected from overmuch introspection. He was eighteen when, by seeming chance, he came across Stewart Macpherson's *The Evolution of Harmony*. Possibly the messenger thought it another Russian novel. At first glance George felt exasperated. Then intellectual curiosity got the better of his irritation. The unknown language of triads, chromatic chords of the seventh, dominant thirteenths, real and tonal harmony bewildered yet fascinated him. He had no piano, no music, no one to reveal the mysteries of this new world. He consulted Ada. She was able to draw a diagram of a keyboard and stave, and to name the notes. His mathematical mind, his sensitive ear, his inborn love of song, and his own determination did the rest. 'I trained myself,' he writes, 'first to set down in musical notation any melody, and then to add a piano score, although I could not use my hands well enough to play a simple hymn-tune. I had been a choir boy and loved singing, so I decided to be a writer of popular songs. I could write a satisfactory piano score and know what it would sound like when played, before I had a piano.' A letter written years later reveals with what tenacity of purpose he set to work: 'All through the year 1921 including the heat wave, I was reading theory of music for about eight hours a day, trying to overcome all the natural and unnatural obstacles to a love of music.'

The self-taught man has a very ignorant fellow for a master, and on the face of it, all his efforts would probably have got George Thomas nowhere. The struggle might have rendered him tough-fibred, but hard, dry and sapless too. However, help was at hand.

PART TWO
The Craft of Writing

CHAPTER FOUR · OUR
MUTUAL FRIEND

1927—1930

As far as the world at large was concerned, the Thomas family had perished from heart and mind. In 1920 the disease had declared itself in the ten-year-old Dan. Physicians here and there showed a professional interest in what was then an unusual case, but the interest did not include food or medicine, although it did lead to an occasional outing of sorts, as when all three children provided the medical students of a neighbouring hospital with an object lesson in the progressive stages of muscular dystrophy. 'We went to the examination because we would get 10/– for it,' George explains, 'real live specimens at 3/4d. each!'

Life would have been insupportable but for books, and those they collected wherever they could. The volumes were almost all in various stages of dilapidation; some they acquired from the second-hand bookstall beneath their window, others reached them as Dad's perquisites from the kindly proprietor of The Newcastle-on-Tyne. When they came to leave Berwick Street they had amassed no fewer than seven hundred and fifty, for books had become a necessity. By reading and re-reading their well-thumbed treasures, George and Ada had begun to discern the existence of a culture beyond their imagining. And then, one day in 1926, like a meteor in the night sky, Erica Oxenham walked into the room overlooking Berwick Street market.

She was taken to visit Ada by a member of the Shaftesbury Society, an organization founded in 1844 for the social welfare of poor and crippled children. The Thomases knew her name by repute, for her father, John Oxenham, the novelist, was then at the height of his career. Erica set out to give sympathy and companionship to one young woman. But life constantly teaches how mysteriously little things are in this world connected with great, and almost without knowing it, she ended by revolutionizing the lives of the whole family.

Every week for the next four years Miss E. as George calls her in his published diaries, climbed to the second floor of the tenement. 'I remember vividly the narrow entrance to the house, pitch dark very often,' she recalls, 'and the uneven narrow stairs, with dark shadows lurking on the landings and in the doorways.' It could be frightening. But once inside, all was transformed. Everything was cheerful, trim and tidy: Ada on the alert, her bright red curls a vivid splash of colour, books for discussion neatly laid out; George, eager and expectant, drawn up closely to the table which supported him and concealed his tattered trousers; Mum on her couch, grey-haired, stout and homely, a silent but interested spectator, her splendid dark eyes full of understanding, wisdom and humour;

and Dan, ever ready to stop a gap with one of his classical stories. For E.O. soon ceased to be Ada's friend only; they one and all took her to their hearts. 'If you hadn't turned up when you did at No. 6,' Ada assured her, 'our heads would have been solid bone by now.'

There was no danger of their brains solidifying. Hours never passed more quickly. George now began to experience that sense of triumph a man naturally feels at an act of the intellect, at conquest of the 'thing' as the mind truly grasps it. Under this new stimulus, he began by asking questions of literature and ended by asking questions of life. The disputations fostered by Erica Oxenham had one direct result: they forced him to write. When the excitement had died down after her departure, he and Ada thought over all they should have said. For days together they would exercise themselves in this literary 'esprit de l'éscalier', but when he urged his sister to send Erica their after-thoughts, she would plead tiredness and there was nothing left but to do it himself. He was thus initiated into an art which was to become one of the main joys of his life: 'I think letter-writing one of the highest forms of human intercourse,' he declares. 'I have built those friendships which I treasure most with Pauline sincerity, postage stamps for bricks, and ink for mortar.'

His earliest letters, written in a large unformed hand, are self-conscious, awkward, and peppered with capital letters, inverted commas, words misspelt, and clumsy syntax. 'Perhaps you would like to meet Mr Howell?' he writes to E.O. 'If you do, and I did not write letting you know when you could, it would be a long time before I could forget that it would have been through my carelessness.' In 1927 Erica proposed that he and Ada should spend a month at Bognor. The prospect of leaving his familiar four walls inspired dread rather than relief. 'Your holiday suggestion is remarkable,' he gravely informed her, 'as an eloquent indication of your very kind disposition towards us, and we will be pleased to talk it over, but I'm sorry, as I think we will not be able to take advantage of your very kind offer. I think it would surprise most people how useless we would be outside of No. 6 Berwick Street.' The day was to come when he would meet a correspondent's grandiloquence with, 'Why do you have to "clothe your ideas in suitable words" before you can express them? Why not do as I do and send them naked and unashamed—the glow about them will keep them warm. Look at the parables—they say all they have to say: "A certain man had two sons"—that's straight enough!' For the moment however Ada might well tease her brother about his 'pedantiquated style'.

Erica Oxenham never tutored George directly. She waited with quiet sympathy while he learned to master his words, and by her choice of subjects and discriminating comments, she brought into light and colour the lines and shapes of thought hidden deep within his own mind. Her letters raised his spirits and fed his intellect during years when all that he knew was that he was locked out of life and cut off from his kind. 'I read your letter at least ten times,' he told her, 'and it came just when it was most needed.' By degrees, he began to make her personal confidences. After a medical examination about this time, he sent her this report:

> Although I enjoyed the change, I am not sure that I did a wise thing in going into hospital; the three weeks spent there have brought me face to face with the stark reality of my condition. The effect is to sadden me more than I care to admit, but it has also given me greater courage, for I clearly see that without that, life could have no meaning for me. For the first time I realize that I have a purpose, which is to justify myself firstly to myself, and then to others.

He grew to dislike the word 'courage' as being 'a word mostly used by the uninitiated to the initiated as a kind of imaginative sympathy'. What he had grasped was that his life would call forth human qualities as heroic as any which distinguish men on a battlefield. It was an important discovery. In a piece of acute and merciless self-assessment he was to admit, half seriously, half in jest, that in the mystery of things his physical condition was possibly the making of him: 'When I think of what I might have been, I see what I have been saved from. Having a mind superficially sharp enough to be clever, I might have been attracted to an easy mode of life. There is one invalid more however, and one less—what? Perhaps I could have been a successful burglar or blackmailer, but I think that having been always interested in politics, I would have had ambitions as a confidence trickster.'

A forced parting from the world had its graces and opportunities as well as its perils. His life might be useless as most men see such things, but he would take care that for himself it had its permanent value. At first he could see its justification only in terms of music. In 1927 his brother Albert acquired a piano, and in spite of useless fingers, arms and wrists, George was able to pick out his own melodies at the keyboard, 'by gravitation as the necessary muscles are absent', he told Erica. His aspirations soared. With the declared intention of publishing them, he took two poems, set them to music, and submitted them for Erica's approval: 'It must pass the test of sincerity,' he wrote to her. 'A composer must turn himself into melody, rhythm and expression, and then if he is sincere, all he needs is a little originality plus a big idea of his own importance (generally called temperament); then after he has been dead a century or so he will be thought a genius, especially if his publishers employ a press agent.' Ada, who was obviously looking over his shoulder, at once condensed her brother's prose into a highly characteristic satirical verse:

Sometimes Fortune favours whom Gods admire,
If he, through lofty thought and high ideals, aspire
To conquer Fate,
And to create
A name
So known to Fame
That each man to posterity doth say:
'His art was great!'
The Fame,
A fitful flame,

54

On him the halo 'Genius' may shed—
If he be dead.

In May 1927 George conquered his fears and went with Ada to spend a month in the little house at Bognor, lent by John Oxenham. The Shaftesbury Society arranged the journey and an aunt accompanied them to look after them. Their mother never left her own kitchen. Like a caged bird, she would not venture into the unknown. For the others, the month at Bognor became a yearly escape into a world of wind and wave, of birds' song, sea mists, and distant horizons viewed through a telescope from the window of their room. 'Our only grievance,' Ada complained, 'seems to be a scarcity of wants.' One day as she and George sat watching boys and girls sway to a dance band, they decided to try their luck with a popular song. Shortly after their return to London, George sent Erica exciting news. A leading music publisher had accepted *With You Beside Me*. The composers did not leap into fame overnight. George was forced to accept the sum of five pounds for sale outright, while three other songs evoked the princely offer of thirty shillings which he refused. Their first success showed them the futility of their ambition; achievement broke their happy dream.

In the winter of that same year, at Erica Oxenham's suggestion, George and Ada enrolled as students under the National Adult School Union. With that, their chains were struck off. They could work, they could run, they had a task to perform, a road to journey, and with trumpets sounding and banners waving, they made a triumphal entry into the kingdom of their own minds. Even Dan, whose cultural interests were confined to hot jazz and detective novels, shared the release from bondage. 'Me and a little Jew-boy down the road are writing a public school story. I've done 25,000 words,' he announced to the family with pride. 'And he hasn't begun to get to the plot yet!' they jeered.

In his first year George followed a course in Psychology, passed to a study of the modern approach to the Bible in his second, and ended up with Philosophy. He showed outstanding ability throughout. 'I feel very honoured,' a tutor wrote to him, 'to have you as one of my students.' The course in Psychology helped him to reach maturity:

I adopted two ideas which helped me by way of analogy and inference: the need of a 'master-sentiment' in life, and the warning to avoid 'over-compensation'. The first helped me creatively, keeping before my mind the need for an integrated life built round an ideal. The warning taught me that integration must not be at the cost of personal subjection to any interest or aim. I might have made an error of judgement in believing that the acquisition of knowledge was in fact education—the making of a personality. It was suggested that I study psychology for some years, as I was a natural student. A little learning is a dangerous thing—but not always. The little I knew rang a warning bell. Here was over-compensation Number one.

I saw myself after those years of study, and I imagined an ordinary working man asking me what

I knew of the world of men and women, of work and unemployment, and politics. And I understood. I was a man whose special task was to wrest some fullness and happiness from life in almost impossible circumstances. I was shut away from life and books would be only half of existence. I need not be a human reference book. I gave up further study of psychology.

With unusual perception, George Thomas had seen that to be a 'clever guy, a know-all' would never solve his special problems or integrate his own life. He accordingly ruled out over-compensations, and psychology went the same way as musical composition and for precisely the same reasons. But what was to take their place and unify his efforts to live a sane and balanced life? It is obvious from his letters to Erica Oxenham that the problem of religious belief had never been far from his mind. He had found that not to believe was too easy a solution. The shrug of the shoulder inherent in Chekov's 'Everything is relative, approximate or conditional' could not satisfy his rational mind. 'In pretending to answer all questions of fact,' he writes, 'it stopped short of the problem of whether it was quite reasonable to suppose such a complex existence as this to be without meaning or purpose.'

So he set to work to rebuild his religious faith, and as he lacked the sophistication which might have taught him to overlook such simplicities, he began at the beginning, at the proof of God's existence from necessary and contingent being. 'There is one thing which one must always be confronted by, and that is, what was the First Cause? Because of my restrictions I would gladly believe there is nothing behind it all, but I cannot, for it leaves only a sense of discomfort, and that in itself is a sufficient condemnation of such an attitude of mind.' As in the physical order starvation had often restored his emotional balance, so now in the spiritual order he found that he could no more do without God than he could do without bread. God was a substantial reality against which no argument had any validity.

George never spoke or wrote without really seeing and feeling, he never relapsed into hollow generalizations or unreal words. Awkward and diffuse as he sometimes is, to the end of his life he continued to dig away in the effort to say exactly what he meant and to mean exactly what he said. What strikes the outsider is the dispassionate eye with which he views things. Life, Teresa of Avila said, is merely one night in a bad inn. Why then, George asks, set great store by the furniture of the hired lodging? Of what account are health and strength, high or low estate, happiness or misery, in the final reckoning? Since they are purely accidental, they neither please nor pain him much. Life, he argues, can only be seen in true perspective when related to the Ultimate:

The real meaning of life is infinity. Death amounts to the end of material existence [he writes to E.O.]. But because I relate everything to God's plan of the ultimate, I consider death no loss. You say, 'I can imagine its being not only a transition but a

58

crashing of one's values.' Exactly; but if one's values are already right, then it is more of a transition and less of a crash. In order to explain God, some base their arguments on natural law, others use human reasoning; both seem to me to overlook the material they use. They are trying to solve an infinite problem by finite means. Both natural law and human reasoning are only applicable to life here. Human reason can conjecture about the reason for *living* but not *dying*. My 'religion' simply comes to this: God does not *send* tribulation but He *allows* it, because He is assured of the final triumph of Good— HIMSELF. I don't care really about conditions here; they are for a time only, and I can prove that Time does not exist—it does not exist because it is useful only for a time! Yesterday was a day like all others of late; I sat in the kitchen growling like a bear with a boil.

The boil was possibly a premonitory symptom of his serious state of health, for in May 1929 he had to spend nine weeks in hospital. Hospitals were to become a recurrent feature of his life, and he found them far from unpleasant. They did much more than merely flavour his days with the spice of variety; they enriched him spiritually. Intensely sensitive and receptive, he assimilated every experience that came his way. Moments were as years, he seemed to dispense with time, and he learned from the strangest masters, even from blindness and anaesthetics. His pleasure in the daily intercourse with three fellow-patients, a doctor, a musician, and an economist, in the small opthalmic ward of St Mary's Hospital, Paddington, was keen and undisguised, but it was not until much later that he spoke of the deeper lessons taught him during that time of outward inaction. He hints at them in two passages in his diary. In the first, he refers to his two weeks' total blindness: 'It was a delightful experience to be blind for two weeks, for in that condition I saw not the figure of the nurse in uniform, but I felt a de-personalized force, which in an inspired moment a biblical writer termed Loving-kindness.' In the second, he was about to yield to an anaesthetic before an operation: 'There was no ambition there nor aspiration but just the condition of *being*. I have no explanation of that, unless it meant something spiritual. I didn't dream it, and yet I had no sense perception other than the experience which Descartes' phrase "I think, there-fore I am" best expresses; just that "I" awareness, and the wondrous beauty of peace.'

Far from interrupting, the weeks spent in hospital had deepened his studies. Every patient there was provided with a Bible, and George made good use of his. Although in his letter to Erica he had theoretically annihilated Time, abstract speculation still left him with the practical problem of how best to use it here and now. It is not surprising then that after rejecting music and psychology he should turn to the Scrip-tures.

My object was to achieve detachment of spirit, and religion became the supreme master-senti-ment. I do not mean that I withdrew from life and prayed for spiritual growth. I accepted the wisdom of the religious view of life because of its truth and practical value. By willingly surrendering the things that would be taken from me by my increasing disablement, I instinctively sought detachment of spirit; for that reason I had a great respect for St Francis, that prince of poverty. I knew I should be literally poor all my life, and I chose also to be poor in spirit, to be free of the possessiveness of things. I was not in search of sanctity. I had to live my life with only the weapons of the spirit for my defence. One does not try to define truth in words, when all that can be seen is the rough path ahead.

As he lacked a Bible for his studies, Sister Anthony gave him a copy of the Vulgate. The contents astonished him. 'Until a few weeks ago', he informed his tutor, 'I had no idea that Saul of Tarsus and Paul the apostle were one and the same person, and I think it as well to admit it.' He became absorbed in this new and exciting study, and read in a very real sense for the fun of the thing. Strangely enough, before enrolling for the course, he had satisfied his conscience that the study would be purely scientific and tinged with no doctrinal bias. Yet he still distrusted authority and wanted to discover for himself a rock-bottomed certainty, a full answer to the riddle of life. He had long ago concluded that this answer was not to be found in reasoned argument, and the Scriptures confirmed his belief. 'How can the suffering of a good man be reconciled with the moral government of God?' his tutor asked during a study of the Book of Job. Here was a grand opportunity for a dramatic exchange of courtesies between the man on the dung heap and the man on the scrap heap.

But there are times, and this was one of them, when a man must make a supreme act of surrender to God or deny Him altogether. The man on the scrap heap was in no mood to waste words. Fiercely he flung back the only reply: 'By Faith and Faith *only*. Human reasoning is a puny thing. Arguments are useless. The problem is beyond human understanding.'

Almost insensibly he was drawn back into the life of the Church. All his theorizing had been divorced from the practical reality of his inmost needs and being. He had never really ceased to belong to the Faith, but to use the old Greek phrase, he had now become what he was. 'I find,' he wrote to Erica Oxenham, 'I am a Catholic at heart with this distinction—I arrived at my conclusions without the help of theology.'

In the winter of 1929 he decided to take the course in Philosophy. Abstract thought involved a discipline at once wholesome and congenial. Not that he was attracted by philosophical theories. He studied Kant, Leibnitz and Spinoza from sheer duty, but there was one philosopher who held him spellbound. Life had taught material detachment, the Gospels spiritual detachment, and now Socrates completed the work with mental detachment:

> Socrates [he writes] inculcated detachment as
> the chief virtue of analysis. By this means man
> could stand apart from himself and hold the scales
> of judgement with unbandaged eyes, not only in
> outward things but towards himself. Then, in the
> final achievement, self-mastery, he would be fit for
> any kingdom.

One might reasonably have supposed that George would be left in peace, fenced off by his four walls from the tumultuous world outside, to pursue his philosophical studies with keen if sober enjoyment. But no; the New Year brought a rude shock. Rumour was rife that the tumbledown house in which the Thomases had lived for almost twenty years was to be demolished. George would need all the detachment that Socrates could impart if he was to bear this unlooked-for trial cheerfully and manfully. The landlord who drew the rents had retired, leaving his tenants to face the situation as best they could. To the fear of removal was added the possibility of a 50 per cent rise in rent which would mean no Sunday joint. With the ever-present consciousness of impending demolition and the pervasive buzz of agitation in the air, George announced that he would like to keep a diary. 'Here you are,' Ada said, as she handed him a thick jotter, 'keep one!' He at once wrote: 'January 1, 1930.—I am going to keep a diary.' He had no other aim but to divert his companions during the trying weeks ahead by reading aloud to them each evening a summary of the day's events, and so provide himself with a basis of fact from which at some future date he could reconstruct a half-forgotten past.

On January 23 the family received a week's notice to quit. George entered in his diary: 'Not having the faintest idea of what to do, Dad intends to ignore the notice and wait to see what happens.' They waited six months. An examination by the 'Insanitary Spectre' as Ada called him, revealed fissures in the Thomases' back wall. On May 5, the housebreakers arrived to remove the roof. The four sat in the little kitchen listening to the thuds and reverberations to which Mrs Thomas's heart beat a responsive tattoo, and to her relief Ada and the two boys were taken off to Bognor. After a month's holiday, the three returned to the indescribable confusion in which they were to live for a further five weeks. Scaffolding shut out the light, the trouble-racked tenants had to fight debris, dust and heavy storms of rain, and amid all the paraphernalia of a disorganized household, George sat on the foot of his mother's bed making laconic entries in his thick notebook:

12 June. The workmen are banging away in earnest up on the roof, and the brick dust and particles are falling in showers. We have a salad today, worse luck.

17 June. Our fears concerning the roof were dispelled as the postman told us that the windows were to be all taken out, but the roof would be left on. The benefit of that news was soon made evident when a terrific storm broke out this afternoon. Soon the water was pouring downstairs on the lower landing, and it was not long before there was three inches of water down there. The noise of the storm had awakened Dad, so he dressed and went downstairs to help. He took a basin, a floorcloth, and a shovel—the latter being the most useful as he managed to shovel up four basins of rain water.

18 June. The old Hebrew woman has a lot of trouble now. Her ceiling fell in as the water got to it from the demolished part of the house, which is on a level with her.

19 June. The boards are back again over the kitchen window, and the only light we get now seems to be a reflection from the wallpaper opposite. The workmen are taking away the wall and soon our window will go the way of the rest of the demolished parts.

24 June. In came the Inspector and a Surveyor, while the Medical Officer stood in the doorway having a good look round but saying nothing. The Surveyor had most to say; he was a kindly middle-aged man with a pleasant face and laughing eyes, and he smilingly inspected the ruins, which included a quick scrutiny of the family, and said, 'Well, it's nice and open for you as long as it keeps fine, isn't it? Did you have any rain last night?' Mother replied, 'No, the rain doesn't come in, and I like this. I don't feel so shut in, and have not had so much air for eleven years, since I was able to walk out in the street.'

28 June. It seems that at every opportunity we must make a joke of our troubles. Deprived of one thing after another, I know now that most things in life are inconsequences, half of the necessities are illusions, and a mind that sees things in proportion is happiest without them.

10 July. Mother always sits on her bed and I sit on the foot also. Ada sits up in a corner by the side of the shoring, which is about eighteen inches inside the room. That causes the kitchen table to be right in the middle of what is left, and with Dan sitting in the corner near the top of Mother's bed, and consequently almost rubbing shoulders with her, there only remained space enough for one to stand in

front of the table. In the space that was to spare, someone had to find room to pack up the contents of the room.

On that day, July 10, the family bade farewell to Berwick Street without regret. 'It will be no wrench to leave here,' George wrote in his diary. 'No other house can witness such frustrations of endeavour, and it is with a feeling of gladness that I look forward to the day when the place will be razed; the memory of it will not haunt me as a mausoleum of lost hopes.' As George was being carried out and put into the taxi, he found himself looking once more into the sad eyes of the old Italian washerwoman whose load he had so often helped to carry as a child. 'She was crying, and somehow although I knew she was pitying us, I felt sorry for her.' His own troubles he could ignore; those of others, never. At length he arrived at 60 Probyn House, Regency Street, where the family was temporarily lodged in a second-floor flat provided for them by the Council. 'Only four walls—but *clean*!' George observed as he studied the topography of his new prison.

When Erica Oxenham paid her first call on them in their new home twelve days later, she found that George was preparing to wind up his diary. The date was July 22, and he remarked that her visit emphasized the fact that they had all resumed their usual routine and there was no reason for continuing the diary. Erica begged the loan of it to show her father. Upon reading it, John Oxenham decided that it would make a book. He at once had the script typed, wrote a Preface to it, and sent it off to his own publishers. They rejected it. People did not wish to read about the troubles of others unless they were crowned with spectacular success, they said. George felt no disappointment. He had known all along the class to which authors belonged. In May 1931, Oxenham tried Jonathan Cape. The book was immediately accepted. 'Mum says she is ever so pleased at my achievement (Yes, she *did* use that very word), also she said "it was a 'orrible exciting moment",' the author reported to Erica. It was months before he gave any hint of his own deeper reaction. Then he wrote to her;

When I knew it was to be published I was overwhelmed, completely humbled, and I was thoroughly unhappy. I got a thrill when I thought how pleased you and J.O. would be; I knew how glad Mum was, but that was all. I felt better after I had received Holy Communion, but nothing I had done justified my feeling happy about the book. Then the proofs came. Since having a direct job to do, I find that in some strange way I am not the person I was before the acceptance. I feel *stronger*— more complete. Like someone who has found a job he has stumbled across, yet which was something he missed without knowing it. I don't think it will make much difference to me except for a sort of rejuvenation. At times I have known a desolation that has been not only mental, spiritual, but almost moral. It is a depression from barrenness. I can't describe it exactly.

Mercifully there was plenty of excitement to occupy his thoughts. Before long the publisher's agreement arrived. 'By the way, you note the paragraph about nothing obscene or libellous,' Erica wrote playfully. 'I'm not suggesting there is anything of the first, but you don't think the old drunk will go and smash Jonathan Cape's windows, do you? I wonder if Mrs Paddie and all Berwick Street will now read the book? On the whole I expect you're relieved that you re-moved Mr Paddie's eighteen black eyes from the story!' 'The old drunk is a saint in the book', George retorted, 'and the people I wrote of cannot be libelled.'

On 12 October 1931, Jonathan Cape published *A Tenement in Soho* or *Two Flights Up* by George Thomas with a Foreword by John Oxenham. Three days later, George's father hurried home from work at half-past six in the morning, silently thrust a copy of *The Daily Express* into his wife's hands, and rushed out again. Opening the paper, she discovered a large photograph of the Berwick Market above James Agate's page-long review entitled 'Diary by a man of great heart'. She called her son and woke him up. Then she tried to read the article aloud but no words would come. Joy had done what adversity could never do. Mum wept.

CHAPTER FIVE · A TALE OF TWO CITIES

1931–1935

'When *A Tenement in Soho* was published', George Thomas writes, 'I was nearly ill with worry about it. I could only think that it would interest nobody, but it hurt to think that I had shown so much of our inner lives to no purpose.' He was wrong. Within four months of publication it was twice reprinted, translated into Dutch, and issued in Braille. Nevertheless reviewers and readers alike doubted its authenticity. One journalist concluded that it was 'propaganda masquerading as a novel'; others assured themselves of the family's existence before committing their views to paper; inquisitive readers invaded their privacy to find out for themselves. Prying eyes however were denied a peep into the living conditions in Soho, for the Thomases' old home was no more, and after a six months' sojourn in Probyn House they moved to a more commodious flat in Victoria House, Ebury Bridge Road. The floors were of stone, the four rooms enjoyed no sunlight, a law of the Council forbade any sitting out of doors, but at least their dwelling was on the ground floor. At first George found the subdued respectability of his neighbours, the unaccustomed calm, and even the patch of green grass in the court-yard, poor compensation for the assortment of foreign faces, the racy adventures, and the human brotherhood of Berwick Market. But now that he was apart from it all, his imagination began to enlarge itself on the past, and he saw in his experience the stuff of a further study of life in a London tenement.

A. Barratt Brown, Principal of Ruskin College, Oxford, who was watching developments with a sympathetic eye, wrote to offer George and Ada a free postal course, and added a word of encouragement to the would-be novelist: 'The novel might do for a Soho neighbourhood what Denis Mackail has done for a middle-class neighbourhood in *The Square Circle*, in which the whole story revolves round the several households in a London Square.'

Thus reassured, George chose his square and his circle. His Square, Crow Court, Soho, midway between Oxford Street and Shaftesbury Avenue is none other than Tyler's Court, Berwick Street, the nursery of his own childhood:

At the farther end a street lamp glimmered, giving the impression that it might flicker out from sheer boredom. The whitewash on the blank wall facing the houses, which was meant to reflect more light into the ground-floor rooms, had a rusty look; it was peeling and falling off in flakes. Old houses, like old churches and cathedrals, had an air of peace or comfort, but here was something different: moribund houses, and people too, with deadened sensibilities.

70

Among the members of the Crow Court circle, two are drawn directly from George's own family. He and his brother Albert were bound by ties of deep if unspoken affection. Three years younger than George, Albert from the age of eleven had shouldered his heavy responsibilities with something of his mother's brains and his father's integrity. He appears frequently throughout George's diary, by turns up to some youthful prank or devoting his day off to household chores, weaving rhymes or concocting plots for detective stories, courting his future wife or quoting *The Deserted Village*. An unmistakable Thomas. This is the brother whom George converts into the hero of his novel, Jim Hunter of the smooth dark hair and bright smiling face, neat, capable, and quick of action, who woos and wins the heroine, Betty Finn.

No less unmistakable is George's youngest brother Alfie, who in *A Tenement in Soho* darts about getting himself off to school, artfully dodges orders from half a dozen people at once, buys all the necessaries, finds time to read and play—and naturally pleases no one but the reader. He stares out of the blue eyes of Tommy Walker, the perky important youngster of fifteen who confides to a sympathetic ear: 'I shan't always be an errand-boy. You stand a chance in *our* firm. We go by what they call seniority and I'll be a foreman some day. Be all right for Ma then. I've only been there a few weeks but I got a boy under me now. Can't order 'im about, you know, but 'e ain't over me, see? That's seniority, ain't it?'

Mrs Grey, the old drunk, the Jewish family from the

first floor, the Paddies, the entire Berwick Street cast is here, and the reader greets them with affection under their thin disguises: Mrs Finn, gone sour before life has had time to sweeten her, sternly managing a husband constantly drunk on borrowed money; the O'Shanes, overshadowed by a poverty that turns the burdened blessing of motherhood into a social crime; Mrs Walker enjoying a six months' respite since 'My old man 'ad a row at the butcher's shop—the copper said it was a haltercation, but I don't think it was one of them—and by accident 'e 'it someone with a leg o' mutton. 'E was a rare one for saying, "I'll 'it yer with it" 'e was.'

Here in unthinkable conditions of overcrowding and under-sanitation, soberly-wise children, apathetic women, and able-bodied men meet each weary day stunted and stupefied by the bleak struggle for existence and the desperate search for work. It is the unforgettable world of the 1930s epitomized in T. S. Eliot's 'Voices of the Unemployed':

> No man has hired us
> With pocketed hands
> And lowered faces
> We stand about in open places
> And shiver in unlit rooms.

The minor characters throughout the book are splendidly alive. Two tower above the rest—Rachel Abrahams, a young Jewess, exquisitely delineated against a thoroughly Judaistic background at a time when many German novelists held everything Jewish up to mockery; and outranking everyone else, the undaunted and indomitable Mary Ann. The author fails badly when he tries to depict virtuous respectability. His heroine, Betty Finn, who returns from the country on the death of her aunt to live in Crow Court, is altogether too altruistic to be anything but a marionette.

In one respect the setting surprises. There are no doss-houses, no street brawls, none of the slum-novelist's usual stock-in-trade. George has planted his circle, not in the over-fictionalized squalor of the East End where West End philanthropy is most operative, but in the heart of Society's London itself. Dispassionately he tells of the poverty, of old coats for bedding, empty cupboards, fireless grates, necessaries of life in pawn, of the washed-out pinafores, symbolic of the washed-out lives. But above, below, or alongside the desperately needy in the four tenements of the Court are families slum-bound from habit or unrepented choice. From one angle Betty Finn, Rachel Abrahams, Ruth and Jim Hunter are slum-dwellers, yet from another these neat and smart young creatures could hold their own anywhere.

Within a year of the publication of *A Tenement*, the novel entitled *Neighbours* was completed. As it went from one publisher to the next, the letters of rejection pointed out that it was not sufficiently spectacular to be a commercial proposition. It lacked change of scene and character, was too objective, there was no clear pattern in the construction of the plot. The author replied that the restriction of setting and restraint of style were deliberate: 'Most of the story is made up of *interior settings*, which speaks for itself. True, I could have written a poster kind of book, but why should I? I write what I know.' Of set purpose he had refused to scarify a slum-depressed area with a muckrake and a fine-tooth comb in order to serve up what was popularly termed a transcript of life. He had written his novel because he had something to say. He wanted to say it as well as he could. The varied criticisms at least opened his eyes to his own incompetent craftsmanship. After the sixth rejection he put his novel on one side and applied himself to the study of technique.

The task lengthened into years. In his new surroundings, George was at least free from the interruptions of Old Misery and the jail-bird. An interval of seven years separates George Thomas's first from his second published diary. They reflect two different worlds. Besides the shifting of the scene, what must strike any reader of both is the alteration in the *tableau vivant*. Mary Ann, Mrs Grey, and Mrs Paddie have given way to Lady Mary Encombe (Lady X), Lady May Ponsonby (Lady Y) and Lady Pauline Kirkpatrick (Lady Z); the names of Mr Murphy and Mr Paddie have been superseded by those of Admiral Mark Kerr, Dr Ravenhill (Mr R), and Father Napier-Hemy, to name but a few of the more outstanding. Many of these friends kept in touch with the family until death or the Second World War separated them. Among them all, Father Napier-Hemy came to occupy a unique place in the affection and lives of the Thomases. On March 11, 1932, George reported to Erica Oxenham: 'This morning Father

Napier-Hemy of the Cathedral popped in with a dog. He had heard from Alec Robertson and had been asked to call by him. He is a great reader and told me to saturate myself in the best books and I would get a vocabulary and style.'

Paul Napier-Hemy, fourth son and seventh of the ten children of Charles Napier-Hemy, R.A. the marine painter, and grandson of Henri Hemy the musician, was aged forty-two at the time of this meeting, and was an assistant priest at Westminster Cathedral. Slight and delicate in appearance, gay, high-spirited and un-conventional, he could adapt himself to all men; whether they were Alfred Thomas or Frank Brangwyn mattered little to him. From their first meeting, he took the Thomases to his heart, as his first letter shows:

Dear George,

Please forgive the familiar mode of address, but how can any one who has read only a few pages of your book address you otherwise? I want to ask your pardon for my temerity in daring to express my views as to how to write—I shall tread with more care in future, for not only do I rejoice in what you say but in how you say it. Thank God you have learned from my patron to suffer fools gladly, so rush in again I will as soon as I can find time, in the appropriate white robe.

Talking about rushing, I escaped from your house yesterday so full of joy, in a hurry to my work, that the children outside thought I was some sort of entertainment and cheered me off the premises. I got no other remuneration: that was more than enough. It is so hard at times to remember one is out of one's teens.

I have one further regret this evening, and it is that 'my customary suits of solemn blackness' forbid me expressing my views in that full rich language with which you are no doubt familiar from its frequent use by your quondam neighbours in the Berwick Market. What I mean to say is, you are a—marvel. Let your imagination supply the epithet I forbear to write.

When I came to see you yesterday I had plenty of work to do, but I doped my conscience by telling myself I was performing an act of charity. Well so I was, but the charity was directed inward and not outward as it ought to have been. Since it is more blessed to give than receive, I am going if I may to receive the lesser blessing, if you will regard me as an object of your charity. Here are the volumes I promised. I hope a little later we shall be able to bring you to the Cathedral for High Mass at 10.30 or if that is too early, for Vespers at 3.15.

One last word before I curl up in bed with my pipe and your book as bedfellows. Please do not think of answering this. Save your pen for words that will one day become immortal (voice in the background from Ginger, 'Ain't 'e shovin' it on, wants to borrer a tanner'). You will see me soon (Ginger again: 'Not too soon, please').

Dear George ('Lor', ain't 'e sentimental, must 'ave 'ad one'), I want to speak of many things.

Goodnight and God bless you all,

Yours sincerely,

Paul Napier-Hemy.

From that day, the priest became their father, counsellor, champion and friend, and many entries in George's second diary show him at his spiritual ministration. This was marked by a whimsicality that cloaked heroic self-sacrifice. Realizing that George needed an outlet, Father Hemy sent him youths to instruct in Scripture and Christian Doctrine. 'I shall die explaining things—if any one is near at hand at the time', the dogmatist writes in healthy self-ridicule. Many of the most striking passages in *My Mind a Kingdom* show the tutor at work with his boy-students, pursuing the scientific methods—the 'pagan approach' as he called it—of his earlier Bible study under the National Adult scheme. The eager little group brought to their task all their human faculties of reason, imagination, and heart. While the atmosphere was strikingly serious, the participants were far from being narrowly sectarian, and the fun could be heightened, for instance, by the piano-tuner's contribution to the discussion: 'I used to read the Bible a good bit, but I didn't like the front part much. It's a holy book, but there were some goings-on them days. You'd be surprised! I couldn't stand their begats and begats, lots of that, but I gave it up after a while; got fed up with their Jobs, Jacobs, Jehovahs and their handmaidens!'

It was part of George Thomas's procedure never to treat doctrines of faith as so many hard and fast canons to which all Biblical texts must conform. The function of faith was not to supplant but to aid the potentialities of the human mind by directing not by stifling it. The Bible's supernatural character as the revealed word of

God he accepted without question, which possibly explains his smiling assertion to a friend, 'My philosophy is not quite Catholic; in fact I prefer a kind of agnosticism or actual paganism, but my priest doesn't seem to mind.' Nevertheless, the moment his faith was really assailed, his action could be both swift and strong. Having concluded that an agnostic member of the study-circle was out to undermine and destroy rather than build up and support, he closed the studies down without further ado. 'By the end of 1935,' he explained later to a friend, 'T.Y. had begun to be deliberately destructive. I stopped the Bible study as it seemed to me a subterfuge for meeting. You'll notice that directly after the holiday—no more Bible talk.' Another friend, admired for his sincerity and goodness, was a dabbler in the occult. His offer to admit George into the secrets of black and white magic likewise received short shrift: 'He believed I held a special office in the hierarchy he knew so well, and that I needed no ordinary initiation, but I said that my church advised mentally weak people to avoid such things. This he greeted with a smile, as I intended he should.' It is not surprising that George's priest exercised a benevolent neutrality towards his 'paganism'.

One day, Father Hemy happened to be present when the postman delivered a letter containing a cheque for £18 for the Dutch translation rights of *A Tenement in Soho*. Handing the cheque to his mother, George remarked: 'Here is another eighteen weeks, anyway.' Mystified, the priest asked what he meant. George explained that since Albert's marriage in 1933, he had made up some of his brother's former allowance by giving his mother £1 a week out of the money he was earning on his first book. Father Hemy thereupon inaugurated a small fund among his friends to augment the family's meagre resources. It amounted to no more than £2 a month, later raised to £3, and anything over and above went into a Reserve Fund for special emergencies. From his first acquaintance with the family, he had wanted to send the invalids to Lourdes and in May, 1934, in response to his application, the Society of our Lady of Lourdes supplied the money necessary to send George and Ada on the English National Pilgrimage to that world-famous shrine. Possibly the recollection of his own instantaneous recovery from brain-fever when at the point of death—an event depicted over the sanctuary in the College Chapel of St Edmund at Ware—led Father Hemy to hope for a miraculous cure.

Physical healing was certainly not the main purpose of George's pilgrimage. Lourdes drew him because, he says, 'I saw that by going to the very place where our Lady appeared, I might gain a glimpse of a truth that could make my religion a living intimate thing.' Much has been written about the mountain-ringed little town in the South of France since the February day of 1858 when 'the Beautiful Lady' appeared in a cleft of the Massabielle rock to the fourteen-year-old peasant girl, Bernadette, as she gathered sticks for firewood beside the river Gave. Rarely however has any pilgrim in George Thomas's state of physical incapacity found strength and expression sufficient to commit his thoughts to writing. If only for that reason, his tiny red notebook, four inches by two and a half, crammed with an almost indecipherable script, has its own value.

For fifteen years he had been debarred from the company of his fellow-men and from participation in everyday life. Now he found himself caught up in the rhythm of the greatest Marian centre of pilgrimage in Christendom, one human being among forty to sixty thousand others, united in one tremendous brotherhood of common faith and aspiration.

> Every one prays for every one else [he writes].
> It seems a place out of this world where there is one
> continuous act of devotion, and where sometimes
> the Spirit of God moves and heals bodies and souls.
> Where one can truly realize the words, 'Go and
> sin no more.' And always there is the spiritual
> inspiration for those who can remember that pain
> and suffering may be the heights and not the depths
> of life.

His day began soon after dawn when he was wheeled to the Grotto. Here at the Lady altar, Mass succeeded Mass like the beads on the rosaries as they slipped unceasingly through the fingers of old and young alike. George lay there seemingly inert but intensely alive as always to the human scene. He notes the workman who, after receiving Holy Communion, an empty bottle sticking out of one pocket and a large narrow hunk of bread out of the other, straightway fills his bottle at the Grotto spring, and marches off to work; he wonders at the shabby little Frenchman who, day after day, stands transfixed in prayer before the Rock, oblivious of the glances of the curious; he is over-whelmed with a feeling of his own unworthiness at the sight of the motionless figure of Dom Francis Izard, monk and doctor, kneeling for hours without support on the bare ground, unconscious of fatigue or the passage of time. The true Lourdes, George decided, as he read his *Daily Express*, was what newspaper repor-ters could never convey. 'The "news" of Lourdes,' he writes, 'is always of cures on pilgrimages, but what Lourdes really does is subjective—not the observed facts of scientific tests, but the unscientific though none the less real discovery of the hidden spring of the waters of faith. Whatever one has to face, by the gift of God and by his providential arrangement, there is nothing —sickness, pain, distress or want—that can compel us to spiritual weakness and capitulation unless we con-sent first.'

George has left a memorandum of talks with two fellow-pilgrims, one in a state of complete rigidity to the knees, the other deaf-blind. They throw a signifi-cant light on the reverse side of the desire to be healed; against the contemporary background of hunger marches and queues for the dole, even the gift of Lourdes had its complications:

> Discussion with Mr L. on the existence of the soul, its significance as a created thing, and man's responsibility to the Creator for the privilege of creation. I could see that he wanted to question whether it was a privilege to be alive in some of the conditions we could see at Lourdes. I gave myself as an example, and suggested that I was probably

making a far better thing out of my life of disablement than I could have done as an able-bodied
person. I quoted:
   'Lazybones, what are you doing there?'
   St Bernadette: 'My job.'
   'And what is that?'
   'Being ill!'
Another time he discussed cures, and admitted that
a cure would have its inconveniences—to have to
face the world anew after thirty years of age. The
blind McB. also wondered what he would do if
cured, and felt embarrassed at the thought of seek-
ing employment in an already overcrowded market.
The desire to work can be as distressing as a disabling
blindness and deafness.

George had already suffered considerably in the
early mornings as he lay shivering in the open air after
Mass, exposed to the piercing blasts which swept down
from the Pyrenees, and the thought of putting himself
into the hands of foreign bath attendants to be plunged
into the ice-cold depths of the miraculous spring filled
him with dismay and apprehension. A conflict between
faith and fear ensued. He refused the baths, until he
suddenly realized that he was shutting himself off
from the full life of the place:

   The bath is a sign of active faith, and from the first
   moment of my five baths, I experienced a lightening
   and brightening of mind and being. Belief takes
   people to Lourdes, but belief of itself is only passive
   receptivity, whereas faith is expressive, volitional
   and dynamic. It is this dynamic quality that one
   receives at Lourdes. The apostles must have ex-

perienced something of the kind on Whit Sunday, and under similar conditions, gathered as they were in one place to pray. Their dynamic belief defied and overcame the world at the expense of what we hold so dear—personal life, but they died that the faith might live—a paradox of human endeavour.

On the last day of the pilgrimage, with something laughing all the time inside him as he put it, George petitioned for his own restoration to health, 'chiefly,' he explains, 'because I had received the benediction of Lourdes in my spirit.' 'Had I been cured,' he told Dr Maud Royden, 'I might be a bigger bounder than I am now.' With eyes lingering on the blue sky above the Rosary Basilica, he left Lourdes and arrived in London as hopelessly crippled after the pilgrimage as before it.

The future seemed as dark and uncertain as ever. His hands, the only tools left to him, were becoming increasingly useless. To write in the normal way would have disabled him at once with cramp; he had just sufficient strength to direct a fountain pen without pressure. 'Sometimes,' he writes, 'I get a moment of special clear-sightedness and I realize that there is nothing, no condition, that really is a help to me. Sometimes I see my hands and know that they are helpless, and it makes me rather subdued—or very angry—with a kind of disgust.'

In spite of his handicaps, with a dogged determination to master his increasing physical weakness, he decided to rewrite the novel laid aside in 1931. Towards the end of 1934 he submitted the completed revision to Lady Ponsonby, who sent it off with a letter of recommendation to her nephew, a prominent member of the publishing firm of Williams and Norgate. On 11 January 1935, Father Hemy, acting as George's intermediary, went to discuss it over dinner with the publisher. As a result, for the first and only time in his many pilgrimages through printer's ink, George received a long letter of constructive advice. The publisher temporarily rejected the book but held out hopes of future acceptance provided irrelevancies were pruned and more work put into the construction of the plot. Following precept by example, with practised pencil he scored through all the redundant and inconsequent phrases of a single chapter before returning the script to its author.

George could now aim at a definite goal however formidable the obstacles. To work at high pressure he needed adequate food and sleep, yet there were times when he went without a drink all day, and sat up all night altering and amending. 'Dad is very good in coming home as soon as he finishes work,' he records gratefully, 'to light a fire and give me breakfast so that it will help me.' No one, except perhaps Ada, appreciated the strain, and the blundering goodwill of obtuse visitors added to his sense of constant frustration: 'The deaf old dear from next door called in, and on seeing me scribbling away thought I wrote nicely. Then she said, "It keeps him occupied, don't it?" The one remark that drives me frantic.' In his daily recital of the ecstasies and miseries of composition, the reader finds himself laughing back at his own reflection in the mirror George holds up to life:

Had the worst row ever with Ada and it has finished our critical collaboration. I do not quite know how these arguments arise but they always end with the family, Mum, Dan, and Ada on one side and myself on the other, which means that, being in the minority, I must be wrong; and always when we discuss the text of my MS. Ada adopts a permanently superior attitude as critic and pontificates accordingly. What decided me to finish the collaboration is that Ada said she only helped me because she was sorry for me. Sorry! I am not sorry for myself. I have no illusions concerning myself, but I do want to write, and I have chosen to re-write this MS., because I believe it is the best way to learn. Where does the necessity for 'sorrow' come in?

The permanent rupture was healed before sundown, and Ada rose next day as unsparing of criticism as of herself. Family dissensions however melted away when Mrs Thomas fell seriously ill during that very week. To play about with fiction suddenly seemed a grotesque parody of real life, and George almost lost heart. Dan undertook the night nursing and for three weeks kept bedside vigil until he could endure no more. He had in fact damaged his heart irreparably although his pluck and humour remained intact. 'If I'm alive to-morrow I'll make my will,' was his parting shot, as he was carried to bed after a bad fall. In other words, George explained, he would leave all his troubles to

Alfie. Ada was taken off to Pinner Hospital for a few weeks' much-needed rest, and no sooner had she departed than George and Dan caught heavy chills. For a whole month the two brothers sat in the living room on either side of the table coughing antiphonally, and fraternizing over port-wine glasses filled with chest and lung mixture while their mother crept slowly back to life.

With Ada's return on April 25, brother and sister resumed their game of battledore and shuttlecock, and on June 14 George put the completed novel into the hands of the publisher. The latter gave it a rapid scrutiny and then, to George's dismay, handed back the last two chapters with an injunction to heighten the romantic theme and tie it up neatly with a lover's knot. For six days George sat staring dully at a blank sheet of paper, his mind stultified by fear of yet another rejection. The publisher's letter of acceptance finally snapped the suspense, and in twenty-four hours George had put the finishing touches to his work. Daisy Ashford herself could not have despatched the dénouement more expeditiously. Within the eloquent space of half an inch between the two sections of the closing chapter, Mary Ann, the arch-conspirator of Crow Court, clears away all misunderstandings between the two young lovers and sets them up happily in a trim little shop in a garden suburb. For good measure, we see her on the last page rapturously inspect their new-born infant, pocket a windfall of ten shillings, and pause at the street corner to wink back in secret understanding at the flickering shop-sign of

J. Hunter and Son, before she trundles home well pleased with the day's work.

During the days immediately preceding publication, the house was inundated by press photographers and publicity agents until even George's father became aware of something unusual afoot. 'At the end of an exciting week,' George notes, 'Dad showed signs of appreciating the tension in the atmosphere. He washed and dressed himself carefully "in case anyone caught him here untidy and unprepared". Mum laughed so much that he went straight to bed.' *Neighbours* was published on October 15. With amusement George studied the headlines of the popular press: 'Triumph for helpless cripple'; 'Achievements of a dustman's son'; 'As a dustman's son sees life'. A few reviewers, ignoring the dust, looked at the artist. 'No one who reads his first novel,' one wrote, 'can have anything but respect, not only for the author's courage, but also for his genius. For here we have the little world which is all the world he can see at first hand, delineated with the accuracy of a Holman Hunt and the inspiration of a Corot.'

Publication brought telegrams, letters, flowers and callers. It was to be expected that more than any other, Father Hemy would share the general rejoicing. He remained indeed as sympathetic and inspiring as ever, but his general governance of the family underwent a subtle change. After Holy Communion he no longer regaled their ears with snatches of song while he prepared their breakfast; instead, book in hand, he sat down and gravely admonished them: 'Take no pride

87

in thy talents or thy wit. Be not proud of thy good works; for the judgements of God are different from the judgements of men.' Reflectively George listened, and afterwards confided to his diary: 'We had Holy Communion this morning; Father H. was in a subdued mood. He read from *The Imitation of Christ* on vanity in worldly things. A warning?'

CHAPTER SIX · GREAT EXPECTATIONS

1935–1938

Although it was translated into Swedish, *Neighbours* was not reprinted. Nevertheless, in the effort of writing it, George had discovered that he was achieving a measure of self-fulfilment so far unknown to him: 'When I am absorbed in writing I am taken out of myself. My helplessness vanishes and is no longer the limiting factor in consciousness. In the warm glow of my mind time does not tick by in minutes, and I feel a wonderful harmony of being. This is partly an explanation of why I write and almost of how I write.'

So he greeted the year 1935 with a fine piece of braggadocio: he would keep another diary, begin a book on Lourdes, plan another novel, and face up to writing as a profession. Taking a large Reporter's Notebook, he entered the date 1 January 1935, and recorded his resolve with a flourish.

His decision to reproduce once again the daily comings and goings of his humdrum life disregarded advice he respected. Father C. C. Martindale, S.J. who had reviewed *A Tenement in Soho* in two long articles in *The Month* discouraged any such attempt. 'You'll find it extremely hard to do a second as good as the first,' he told him. 'Either one uses one's experience or one's imagination. Your experience, I fear, will be less varied than it was, simply because you are more comfortable; your conditions are not so romantic from the public's point of view as Soho was. And I do not know whether you have or haven't imagination. Well, I think you have; but imagination needs food. You can't write your own life *twice*.' But George could be inflexible. He considered the diary form his most natural and effective mode of expression. None knew better than he how physical discomfort could hinder continuity and development of thought, whereas terse jottings lent themselves readily to lively incident and occasional reflection. He set to work.

Many readers of *A Tenement in Soho* had asked its author for further portraits of his family. With quiet enjoyment George turns a spotlight on his father in the act of serving Christmas dinner:

> We heard the King's speech, an intimate, almost affectionate address. Dad always stands to attention when 'The King' is played, and it was no exception today. In fact we had two lots of loyalty and respect in one, as the next item on the wireless was the National Anthem from Bournemouth. Dad stood it through, holding a dinner in hand; but while he did so, Dan found a medal to pin on his chest. It was Dan's dinner he held.

In Pimlico as in Soho, Dan wears his Shakespearian cap and bells with admirable verve and persistent purpose, outjesting his injuries and transforming the family afflictions from tragedy into comedy day after day:

> This afternoon Dan had a bad accident. In the scullery the dinner wagon was in the wrong place, close to the sink, and just beside Dan who was peeling potatoes. He slipped, one leg went under the sink and the other under the wagon. Dan fell backwards but held on to the edge of the sink with one hand. Back and back he went, the weight of his head straining his curvature and threatening to choke him. His head and his posterior met near the floor and almost in the same place. He managed to call out once, and Ada hearing the strain of strangulation in his voice went to him as speedily as she could, with due consideration for her own safety. Drawing a box near, she sat down and grabbing him by the hair tugged until the pressure was off his throat. . . . Father H. came in having heard of Dan's fall. He petted him a good deal, partly in fun, and Dan, who had now recovered his usual nerve, said: 'Do you know, Father, although I don't expect you to believe it, I was sitting on my head when Ada pulled it away.' Father H. made us all grin with his reply, 'Very sensible of you, Dan, to choose a nice soft spot to sit on.'

There are moments when, true to his role, from being a figure of fun or pathos, the jester rises to noble heroism:

> We waited for Dan to come home expecting him to be rather tired and talkative. When he did return he was carried in by the man living next door. He sat very still without saying a word. Mum began

questioning him, and I suddenly shook my head at her frowning a warning to leave him alone. The place he had visited was the orthopaedic home at Pinner. He looked up slowly and said, 'I'm not really tired . . . I've been thinking.' We could not interest him in our demand for tea. He lit a cigarette and in decided tones announced, 'Mum, if I ever grumble at what is wrong with me, I shall deserve kicking.'

Occasionally George's laughter becomes tragic, yet it is never bitter; it is only through laughter that he allows himself to weep. Young Paddie, son of his old friend the jail-bird, though willing to accept even a boy's wages, had spent months in a fruitless search for work. 'When you're after a job,' he complained to George, 'you can't tell them you are twenty or nine-teen 'cause on your card it says you are twenty-five, and they say you are *too old*.' 'I wonder,' his listener asked with prophetic foreboding, 'when young men will be too old at twenty-five for war?' At last the idler strikes lucky:

Young Paddie called to tell us about his job. It is awful. He works at a wharf and has to carry two-hundredweight sacks of soda up a steep stairway into a room, where the ceiling is so low that he has to bend his knees to enter, and then gradually empty the sack into a vat where the steam nearly blinds him. The acid burns his hair and rots his clothes; I wonder what it will do to his eyes in time? He told us why he left work early today. 'I walked in and said "I'm going to 'ave a tooth out" and the guv'nor said "Righto," so I put me coat on and walked off. You know, the tooth was nearly driving me crazy all day.' He went to the dentist and had gas. 'Oo! I went right past the moon. It wasn't 'arf fun. Just as I was going on the moon the bloke said, "Come on—step down." He asked me where I'd been, and I said, "Oo, you couldn't go there, I went past the moon." ' Apparently the dentist laughed, I know we did. Ah well, life has its compensations.

Unlike Tommy Walker's, however, the astronaut's job had no future. Nor had he. When war came, even twenty-nine was not too old. The jail-bird's only son died on his way home from Korea during the Second World War.

There is this notable quality about George Thomas's second diary: the craftsmanship is more accomplished, the writing easier and more assured. It would be incorrect to imagine that he wrote it in the same casual way as his first. Its variety and brevity were not achieved without profoundly conscious art. The work is a fine piece of composition in which the accumulation of detail builds up into an astonishingly accurate and vivid picture of the life around and more especially within him. He never exaggerates a highlight, never omits a gradation. Tragedy shades off almost imperceptibly into comedy, social and domestic trivialities are happily blended with intellectual reflection. Whereas *A Tenement in Soho* had depicted a life rich in Dickensian personalities living under appalling social conditions, *My Mind a Kingdom* rivets the reader's attention almost entirely on the writer himself. The picturesque abounded in the first book; it is completely absent from the second. 'I knew no one in or about Victoria House who was in the least interested,' George wrote in 1938, 'and I had no means of getting to know people. I went from my bed to my chair and my chair to my bed most days.' But however much he might be living in isolation, he was not living in a vacuum.

The deep reflective quality of *My Mind a Kingdom* must strike even the most cursory reader. Over and over again the author's thoughts return to consider the three mysteries that most concern and perplex man's mind: life, love and death. There may be nothing startlingly original about his ruminations, but his words compel attention because they are the words of a man who, as one soon realizes, has lain many a night in the dungeon of Giant Despair. Yet with the first rays of the morning sun he has plucked up heart, grasped once more the key of promise and turned his back resolutely on Doubting Castle. His is no comfortable armchair philosophy. Is suicide in debate? There is no problem to discuss, he replies, unless life and death have a value and purpose beyond human comprehension. As for himself, he can discover his equilibrium of soul only in marching and continually marching: 'I have not found life a great adventure but mostly an unbearable trial, and the only thing I know for certain is that I have to go on. I have often thought of giving up the struggle but as long as I can do anything at all, I must do it. And so it comes about that I enjoy most things, even the fight.'

The mystery of life and death brings him up against

the problem of human love, that most powerful of all the tried and solid things which help a man to live and die. The invalid condemned to sit immobile from morning to night with spine incapable of support, face incapable of laughter, hand incapable of friendship's grasp, turns aside for a few moments from his study of *D. H. Lawrence: A Memoir,* to demolish with a chill blast of commonsense what he considers its sophistry:

> D.H.L. and E.T. read Schopenhauer's essay on 'The Metaphysics of Love', and D.H.L. had written 'Maggie Tulliver and Philip' in the margin against this passage: 'The third consideration is the *skeleton*, since it is the foundation of the type of the species. Next to old age and disease, nothing disgusts us so much as a deformed shape; even the most beautiful face cannot make amends for it.' Schopenhauer wrote of metaphysics on an entirely physical plane, and as if Love is a physical quality instead of a metaphysical thing with physical repercussions. People do not love skeletons nor the meat on the bone. There must be truly a quality which is above physical properties. There is far more mystery in the metaphysics of love than in any 'third consideration' postulated by Schopenhauer. Perhaps I should agree with him if I were not deformed, but I find that neither my disease nor my deformity 'disgust' people. Love is more than anything purely physical, for life itself is more than existence.

And what if circumstances kill the love that once seemed imperishable? One December evening as George sat listening to Clemence Dane's *A Bill of Divorcement* over the wireless, he heard from across the years the voice of Amy, a twelve-year-old playmate, saying to him: 'Give me that ball, and I'll be your sweetheart for ever!' 'Even children recognize the essential,' he reflected. 'One would hardly expect a love-token to declare constant or even possible change.' Love cannot be offered subject to conditions; it is a matter of eternal responsibility and true growth—and growth necessitates pain. That night he entered in his diary:

We found *A Bill of Divorcement* good but in some ways unsatisfactory. If love comes to a man or woman who is tied to an insane person, they will find a way out of the difficulty however moral they may be. The whole problem is one of suffering. People think it evil that any one should suffer, but such an evil, unlike pleasure, does not surfeit. It helps one to grow in the fullest sense. It seems unreasonable to me to expect a world to contain happiness that does not also contain sorrow—they are the poles of experience, and much nearer to each other than they seem, for at the dividing line they touch. I always suspect that the greatest human weakness is not vice but self-pity, and 'suffering' in the ordinary sense is that kind of weakness; when the time comes, one discovers that one can endure prodigies of real suffering of a kind that, while it hurts, helps one to understand the greater glory of the even tenor of existence, that unappreciated level which so easily sways towards joy, peace and beauty.

Is love then all-sufficing and all-sufficient? Does not

experience teach that however tender our love, however much we may desire to share in the life and destiny of another, complete exchange is impossible? The insulation is merciless. Incapable of breaking the bonds of 'I' and 'You', we escape one another at every moment, and at the end must face life's supreme act alone. Does the paradox imply an inherent contradiction? In a letter to a correspondent unable to believe in life after death, George Thomas strives to express his conviction that all things are one, that however separate and disparate they may appear, they are in fact all moving in strict time upon the rich harmonies of Divine and human love. The letter concludes:

> We are created as self-contained units and exist within our own personalities, cut off from outward things as completely as though nothing else existed but ourselves. This isolation is the primary law of being and it is *deliberate*—we were made that way for a special purpose. All the mistakes and unhappiness in the world are caused by attempts to break through the barrier in the pursuit of our idea of happiness or good. They fail unless they are attempts within the sanction of the plan. The whole point is that once we believe that there is a plan for us, the question of whether there is immortality or not fades out as an argument.

Shortly before his death, as William Morris sat in his study at Kelmscott House overlooking the Thames, a tear or two trickled slowly down his cheeks. Suddenly aware of being observed and anxious to forestall consolation, 'An old man's tears are not always tears of sorrow,' he remarked, 'I was thinking of things I could tell to no one.' And there he spoke for Everyman. There are things we could not tell if we would, would not if we could. The tension thus engendered between our need for sympathy and our undeniable isolation at times makes human existence almost unendurable. Many run away from themselves by filling the solitude with noise, an evasion which becomes ever easier in a world like ours where space resounds with the roar of traffic, where silence is considered unproductive void, where radio and machine invade and envelop, strangling speech and stifling thought. Others, fewer in number, go to the opposite extreme. Sad and frustrated, they withdraw into themselves, finding in a stoical acceptance of the inevitable, the bitter—but not necessarily the best—response to the enigma.

When George Thomas propounded his solution to this problem, he packed into a single entry under the date May 8 in *My Mind a Kingdom,* the personal experience and meditation of six long years:

The significance of life, to my mind, is clear. Pain, suffering, sickness, cruelty; if we look at life we can see that all those things that worry and grieve us have their importance because death, not life, is the problem. Why should some people or animals suffer and others not suffer? What have I got that makes me happy even now? There is one fact, I think, that few ever suspect. A human being is in a state of isolation that defies all efforts at breaking through. The individual consciousness seeks for contacts with others, and believes it achieves true contact, but it is a deception. Subjective isolation is a law of creation. I asked myself, 'Why do people seek for contacts with others that when apparently attained never satisfy?' Because the isolation is the primary condition, and the proper contact is the fulfilment of being. How many varieties of contact are there? Only two, I believe. We try one, naturally, but do not always attempt the other. Being isolated, we must relate ourselves to the Source of Life to find a reason for the isolation. But instead, we search the world for a way out of our isolation; no one has yet broken through in that way. People think that human love solves the problem, but it does not do so alone. Once admit that isolation is the natural state of the soul, and one at once sees that to break through this isolation we must turn to God first. It then seems as if the isolation were a protective barrier given for our own spiritual well-being. This isolation is one of the conditions of 'Thou shalt love the Lord thy God' and *then* 'thy neighbour as thyself'. I know nothing else as simple. One sees God everywhere as St Francis did, present in His work, and His greatest work is 'thy neighbour'. Live to that plan and there is no isolation; relate everything to the Source and Sustainer of everything (even human folly), and there remains no mystery. 'The Hound of Heaven' is one aspect of the situation.

In this specifically Christian solution, no fact of human existence has been changed, there is no loosening of the bonds of reality, no mysterious esoteric doctrine of inner experience or renewal; man's talents, health, hardships, limitations remain what they were, yet they have been radically transformed. No longer is human isolation looked upon as an invulnerable circle complete in itself like a snake with its tail in its jaws. By accepting the implications of 'the primary condition' the ring is broken simultaneously from within and without. For God is no mere psychological, moral or religious concept. He is Absolute Being, and when he made man, God implanted in him both the need and the capacity for none other than Himself. Therefore, George Thomas points out, the only gateway out of the tangled world of illusion is for the creature to make the Creator the foundation of his existence.

Whether the world at large would be prepared to share his vision was quite another matter. The time had come to put it to the test. The diary begun on 1 January 1935 ran out on New Year's Day 1936, for no better reason than that it marked the end of the calendar year, and with no more dramatic ending than Albert's settling into the same block of flats. The chronicle of events in bare outline could hardly be called romantic or sensational. It would run something like this: Mrs Thomas keeps her fifty-fifth birthday, is wheeled to a cinema where she enjoys her first talkie, falls ill but recovers; Dan goes on pilgrimage to Lourdes and returns as he went; George tells us what he ate for dinner, what for tea, notes with scrupulous exactitude every guest and every gift, publishes his first novel, and as a result is invited to speak on the B.B.C. programme 'In Town Tonight' for two minutes forty-four seconds. On the face of it, the monotony of such trifling to and fro is undeniable; today differs so little from yesterday and the day before. Had Father Martindale been right? Did a flat in Pimlico lack the popular appeal of a tenement in Soho? But there was far more to it than that. George knew that his second diary was on a different plane and demanded different standards of judgement from his first. Without forwarding it, he wrote to ask Mr Jonathan Cape whether he would consider a sequel to *A Tenement in Soho*, but was disheartened to receive the reply: 'Full up for a year ahead.' So he had no alternative but to try elsewhere.

The year 1936 came and went, punctuated only by the periodic return of the same pre-paid registered package, and New Year's Day, 1937, dawned on a seemingly arid future. In spite of the proverb, coming events cast no shadow.

Two days later Mr J.S.L. a London businessman of wealth and influence sent a letter c/o Messrs Jonathan Cape to John Oxenham. In it he explained that having recently read with great interest *A Tenement in Soho*, he wished to find out whether there had been any amelioration in the painful condition of the Thomases' lives. He was avoiding a direct approach to the author of the book, for fear of being suspected of impertinent curiosity. John Oxenham put the matter into his daughter's hands, and over a meal Erica and J.S.L. reviewed the situation. As he discharged a volley of questions, J.S.L. made lightning decisions. The Thomas family must be established in simple but real comfort —could he meet them? Accordingly on January 22 he and Erica Oxenham picked their way through the puddles to No. 7 Victoria House, Ebury Bridge Road. He there plunged straight into a discussion of their food, income and expenditure, spoke of making their future secure, and told them that justice demanded they should receive their fair share of the total income of the nation. Language such as this was of course completely foreign to the Thomases' mentality. However they accepted it since it looked as if the black cloud that had always overhung their future was to be lifted for ever, and to none did it bring a greater sense of relief and gratitude than to Mrs Thomas. J.S.L. immediately used his influence to get the family a larger and sunnier flat, and within a few weeks had secured one pleasantly situated on the ground floor of a newly-built block only a short distance away. For the rest of the year his benefactions in the way of structural alterations, food, flowers and furnishings were many, but probably his most generous was the provision of a housekeeper with some nursing experience to ensure the invalids prompt meals and necessary medical attention. In return, his secretary supervised their accounts—a dangerous assignment. The situation clearly contained germs of misunderstanding from the outset.

When J.S.L. offered George some book-reviewing, the latter could only urge his incapacity to work to schedule, but at the back of his mind there was another factor. Was he competent to fulfil such commissions? For no sooner had he settled into his new surroundings than the postman delivered an all-too familiar parcel.

It came from a literary agent: 'I am afraid we cannot undertake the negotiation.' George re-read his script. The further he went, the more certain he became that the book was worthwhile. In his perplexity he decided to ask Miss Victoria Sackville-West, who had given his first diary high praise, if she would give him her honest opinion of his second. Three days after receiving the MS. she returned it with an Introduction in which, for the benefit of author, publisher, and public alike, she marshalled cogent reasons for retaining the diary exactly as it stood. With such a preface, publication was assured. George sent it off at once to Jonathan Cape, who accepted it within a week.

No one was more proud of 'Lawyer Thomas' than his mother. With unaffected delight she looked out for letters and reviews. One appreciation touched her more than all the rest. It came from a lawyer whom the publishers had consulted while the book was in proof stage:

I want to tell you [he wrote] how deeply I appreciated the book—particularly the passages dealing with your Faith. I have been corresponding with a friend who was ill and troubled. I had sent her *The Imitation of Christ*. She found it helpful but couldn't 'accept about the *creatures*—because one wants to love visible, tangible humans rather than an invisible intangible God'. I copied out and sent her an extract from your diary (May 8, from 'The significance of life . . .'), and she has written in reply: 'I think it's one of the clearest, best things I've ever read.' I am sure the book is going to help many. A lawyer's blessing on it! You wanted to be a lawyer and have become a writer. I wanted to be a writer ...'

The proofs were hardly completed when George was taken seriously ill. His voice scarcely rose above a whisper, and septic eyelids deprived him of the joy of reading. Greatest hardship of all, he was out of reach of his mother, and lay the space of two rooms away, unable to move without help. Towards Christmas Mrs Thomas herself became alarmingly weak, and she sat day after day in the living-room on a divan, propped up with pillows and fighting for breath.

January 14, 1938, brought the publication of *My Mind a Kingdom*. That evening Mrs Thomas was so exhausted that Dan decided to watch throughout the night at her side. Next morning she admitted that her strength was no more and asked if the family could procure a nurse. But she was the last person to allow her own indisposition to cast a shadow over their joy, for with the appearance of five press notices of George's book in leading dailies that morning, things had worked up to a high-water mark of excitement. At one o'clock Mrs Thomas asked to re-read the reviews, gave instructions as usual about the flat and the morrow's food, handed over her workbag to Ada, watched her set the contents in order, and at 4.30 lay down, unable to rest or sleep. Dan, with a premonition that something was seriously amiss, had already summoned doctor, nurse and priest. The doctor's diagnosis was grave. The family roused their father and sent an urgent message to recall Albert from work. Before leaving, Dr Carter went along to George's room. 'Do you think we could let him get up to go along to the living-room this evening?' he asked Jill, the housekeeper. Something in the quiet tones and the oblique question warned George that his mother was mortally ill. Until that moment he had never suspected the truth. Jill wheeled him to his mother's side. Presently Albert rushed into the room and fell on his knees as Father Eugene Langdale anointed the now-unconscious figure and led the prayers for a departing soul. 'I said the prayers with the priest,' George wrote afterwards, 'and was there when Mother died an hour later. She died without a hint of unwillingness or sorrow. I could never hope to see a more peaceful passing.'

There was one notable absence that evening. Grief-stricken at his separation from the family at such a time, Father Napier-Hemy did his best to comfort them from the Nursing Home where he was slowly regaining his shattered health:

Dearest Friends,
   God knows best. I can't write, only cry. That heroine is now at rest. Please ask Father Langdale to offer four Masses for her. I thank God she knew of your triumph before she was called. Dante says, 'Sorrow re-marries us to God.' This is a great grace for you all because it will bring you nearer to God. My illness has told me one thing: God alone matters. Mum's death is His way of tenderly telling you, 'We have no abiding city.'
   Tell Father Langdale I hope that her body will lie before the altar the night before the Requiem.

I want everything done properly. You can't even
go, but lots of people will be there. She must have
a grand funeral because she was grand. R.I.P.
                    Love to all,
                        Paul Napier-Hemy.

The undaunted trio who had surrounded their
dying mother felt little distress in the accepted sense
of the word. True, a future without Mum was, they
conceded, Hamlet without the Prince. But they were
not thinking of themselves. Their joys had always been
doubled by seeing them reflected in her eyes. It was to
his mother that George had handed the first copy of
his new book fresh from the press. She had lived to
see it acclaimed. Her son was content. He knew that
she had died on the crest of a wave. That was his real
success.

PART THREE
The Craft of Loving

CHAPTER SEVEN · LOSS
AND GAIN

1938–1941

On 16 February 1938, a month after his mother's death, George was sitting alone wishing she were alive to witness the signing of an American contract for the publication of *My Mind a Kingdom* when he suddenly found himself in the presence of Queen Elizabeth (the present Queen-Mother), who had decided to pay an unexpected call on the residents of the new block of flats. Seated on a divan, she told him with what interest the King and she had read his first diary. Meanwhile, unconscious of his sovereign-Lady's presence beneath his very roof, Dad, honest patriot though he was, lay fast asleep in an adjoining room. By the time he rose for his evening breakfast, her Majesty had come and gone; the train of press photographers, the chatty reporter from the *Daily Mail,* the pair of seasoned old hands from the *Daily Sketch*, the smart young woman from the *Daily Express*, and the quiet young man from Sheffield on his first London assignment had all departed; and Dad was free to enjoy his meal in peace regaled only by his family's anecdotes of the day's adventure.

'I cannot see anything happening to us now of an epoch-making nature,' George wrote that same month. 'Mother has gone, and the Queen calls only once in a lifetime.' Within four weeks, on March 12 1938, Hitler's storm troops had marched into Vienna, the Austrian Republic was annexed to the German Reich, and the air of London was heavy with dark hints and terrifying whispers. Gas masks were to be issued to all citizens and plans for air defence were hurried on. With nerves worn fine by sinister rumours and intense moral stress, the Thomases sat listening to the wail of sirens. George's overspent body then retaliated and he collapsed under the strain. It was not that he lacked human sympathy; it reached him from all sides and from the most unexpected quarters. The editor of *The Spectator*, for instance, suggested a series of articles based on interviews held in George's own home with people the editor would appoint, but George would not hear of it. For perhaps the only time in his life, he was destitute of courage and refused the generous offer.

He based his rejection on his inability to meet the obligations such work would necessarily entail. There was however another fact, possibly unrecognized at the time, yet subtly potent in effecting the change that came over him during the next three years. Among the papers he preserved, there is a sheet containing four short poems. One of them bears the date 1937:

> When I am sore
> (Such is ingratitude),

Hold wide the door
Of your beatitude;
Disclosing there the glowing evermore
Of love unborn;
Revealing there a rose, where but before
Had been a thorn.

In his youth, Mrs Thomas had warned her son against mistaking pity for love. He had accepted the admonition at the time, but in fulfilling his resolution to live a life as nearly natural as possible, he decided that his emotional life must be free even if eventually denied. On 2 April 1938, he entered in his diary: 'M. came for the last time before going home for the summer. A good friend. We shall miss her. Everyone here is fond of Ada's friend.' The understatement of the last phrase will be obvious to anyone familiar with *My Mind a Kingdom*. However much her friendship may have embraced the whole family, the book makes it clear that George's mind was the magnet that drew her. They had met in 1932, and for the first time in his life George found a friendship based on frank equality. In the abnormal circumstances, Margaret N. came to symbolize for him that 'glowing evermore of love unborn' of which his poem speaks. But her goodbye on 2 April 1938, had in it a finality which both secretly recognized. She revisited the family occasionally, but never again on the old footing. The loss of her companionship brought on a crisis which was as much psychical and emotional as physical in origin. The cryptic poem dated 1938 is more than a literary exercise:

Words are vain,
Tears are pain,
Love has bled:
Tears are vain,
Words are pain,
Love is dead.

'I think my unhappiness began then,' he confessed later. The accumulated burden of his mother's death, Dan's heart weakness, the suspension of Father Hemy's visits, added to his own loneliness, his ruined health, and the uncertainty of the future were all of course contributory factors. Such however being the complexity of man, the crisis assumed the outward form of a revolt against his ancient enemy—religious authority; but one suspects that the protest was George Thomas's attempt to rationalize and lend dignity to what was essentially an emotional conflict.

He was fond of saying that if he was still a Catholic, it was by the grace of God and his own efforts. Up to a point that was correct. As early as 1931, writing in *The Month*, Father C. C. Martindale had drawn the attention of Catholic welfare workers to the bad psychology which underrated intellectual and material needs, and hoped to reach the soul while ignoring mind and body. Selecting George Thomas as an object lesson, he pointed out that but for his elementary school grounding in the Penny Catechism, the young man's faith must necessarily have gone by default save by a miracle. In attributing its preservation however largely to 'self-help'—his own phrase—George was running the risk of imagining that even spiritually he could claim to be a self-made man. And what self-made man bows humbly to authority?

Ironically enough it was precisely the Catechism learnt by heart in the tiny school in Dufours Place which made him hoist the rebel flag. The Penny Catechism, the basic training for centuries of all English-speaking Catholic children, has an illustrious parentage. It has been indebted in turn to St Peter Canisius' Catechism of 1554, the Doway Catechism of 1649, and to such distinguished revisers as Challoner, Manning and Ullathorne. In this century opinion as to its merits has been sharply divided. Whereas a famous headmaster of Downside considered Caesar's Gallic War, the Rule of St Benedict, and the Penny Catechism to have been the three most educative forces in Europe others, more especially since the Second Vatican Council, see in it nothing more than a collection of abstract frozen formulas unconnected with the life of the Christian soul, unfortunate in terminology, and calling for drastic revision.

In 1938 George Thomas resumed a study of the Catechism in the light of his adult experience. All went well for a page or two until at a certain point his amused familiarity with the text turned into an explosive doubt. These words met his critical scrutiny:

Question: What are the three powers of your soul?
Answer: The three powers of my soul are my memory, my understanding and my will.

This classification, derived from St Augustine, has puzzled many a thinking reader. It may be sufficient to point out here that the term 'memory' is to be equated at least partially with what we should call the 'unconscious' or the 'subconscious'.

Faced by the difficulty of the terminology and acting on his principle of 'Question everything', doubting Thomas thought rapidly: 'If God directly creates the human soul with the power of memory, then the soul must retain knowledge of its origin, and no soul in possession of three such powers could possibly sin with full deliberation against God its creator.' He ended by calling into question the whole doctrine of original sin and man's Fall, and spent the next three years banging his head against the high brick wall of the Catholic Church's teaching authority.

From one point of view his attitude is not surprising. He had been cut off since boyhood from all exterior participation in worship, and during the groping years of adolescence had lacked even elementary guidance. With his awareness of Divine realities, he had never been able to doubt God's existence and overruling providence. The claims of Christ to be God were another matter. He had deliberately foregone his childhood's faith and dispassionately subjected these claims to examination. The moment he accepted them without reservation, life had taken on new dimensions. But he had one more step to take. Catholic theology has three points of light, not two: God, Christ, the Church—not in juxtaposition like three links in a chain, but inseparably one. God is revealed and accessible to us only through Christ, Christ only through the Church. Nor is the Church superfluous once it has led a soul to Christ, any more than Christ is superfluous once He has led a soul to God. George Thomas had yet to discover the Church: to him it was nothing more than an exterior institution, a human organization rather than a Divine organism. When therefore the world as he knew it came toppling about his ears and he began to reassess his values, it was against the Church that he drew his largest note of interrogation.

At this juncture Mary Tiernan crossed his path. She had chanced upon his two diaries in June 1938, and on her way through London to the Isle of Wight the following month, had sent him flowers and a letter to say how much she appreciated his work. On July 22 she received from him an invitation to call if she so wished on her way back to Dundee. She did not do so, but sent several gifts of flowers at intervals and a further letter in September. It was not until the following January that George replied, pleading in excuse for the delay his anxiety over his twenty-two-year-old brother Alfie. The youngster who appears so often in *A Tenement in Soho* bubbling over with mischief and vitality had completely escaped the family disease only, it was feared, to lose his life in a motor collision at midnight in Victoria. 'But you can't squash a Thomas,' the boy remarked cheerily, when after six weeks' unconsciousness he returned to life. For nearly two years he was to share the immobility of his sister and brothers, and learn maturity and prudence in the same stern school. 'Alfie was in an accident in June and nearly died,'

George explained to Mary Tiernan. 'At present he is disabled—"one of us".'

Believing that her correspondent was a fervent Catholic, Mary mildly protested in her next letter against George's disparagement in *My Mind a Kingdom* of a French girl's immediate response to a religious vocation. Diffidently she asked whether the girl was not in duty bound to answer God's call, cost what it might? She can hardly have been prepared for his reaction:

> The entry for March 25—the 'vocation'. I suggest that a vocation is a matter of temperament, that is, fundamentally a question of glandular function; and a religious vocation is no different from any other. I think that you don't even suspect the ideas that are held today in some quite respectable quarters. As a Catholic your technique of living is not your own, but a series of habit formation compulsions. If I shock you as a Catholic you must forgive me. I've had a hard fight and I've not been able to keep my end up merely by following a pattern set by someone else. I had to take responsibility for 'my soul' upon myself and work *towards* a spiritual interpretation of life. I don't expect you to agree with me, since what is effective for *you* is all that matters for your ultimate good. And there is the explanation of 'vocation' too!

At no time in his life perhaps would Mrs Malaprop have eulogized George's observance of the social niceties as being the very pineapple of politeness, yet the open discourtesy is surprising. On the surface, the events of the year had certainly proved exhausting. Like thousands of other Londoners, George had spent months trying to find a refuge in the Home Counties should war break out. Early in 1939 a friend, Miss V. M. Jones, discovered a vacant bungalow in Guildford. She and a kind Jewess, Mrs Peter Harris, put their heads together: one agreed to pay the rent, the other to provide furniture, linen and the rates. All was finally settled when George and Dan set out in March expecting to stay four months. They stayed for six years.

Externally life showed little change. 'I am alone most of the time,' George wrote to Mary Tiernan on March 23, 'because I sit in my room which is too far for me to get to the other room without strain, and I seldom use a wheel chair.' Neither the spring sunshine nor the roses and chocolates which accompanied her Easter greetings warmed him into affability. Her obvious wish to continue the discussion on religious vocation met with prompt rebuff:

I'm not inclined to argue with you about vocations or anything else. I have a satisfactory method for myself, but it would be wrong to think of me as a 'soul perfectly at peace'. Every day is a nuisance, and I'm *damned* helpless. Please don't quote the Bible and don't argue. I'm writing today instead of being in the sun only because of the greater concentration obtainable in writing letters as dope to keep me more or less normal. After all, I've kept you waiting a week deliberately, so why should I write on a sunny day? Ah, I know: I've begged the question—I'm not normal!

Whitsuntide came. Unruffled by his rudeness, she sent a gift of fruit, chatted about a recent trip to Edinburgh, and asked him casually why he refused to argue. 'I believe you are a good Catholic', he told her, 'and I wanted to avoid anything that might not fit in with your harmonious religious practice.' Then forgetting his resolution, he erupted: ' "O happy Fall to merit such Redemption" is sentimental rubbish. Authority likes the idea of controlling us all because we are "sinners". Who says we need a Church and its Authority? The Church! We are all educated on the understanding that we must do as we are told, but in fact social forms of control are makeshifts, because civilization comes in the middle of the human story and not at the beginning. Don't let us argue. You see, I am not a "charming person"—more like a purple revolutionary. But I am *me* (excuse the grammar) and not a hotch-potch of other people's ideas.'

Avoiding polemics, the tactician asked him to tell her about Lourdes and urged him to publish an autobiography. But he was in no mood to be placated:

About Lourdes: you ask four definite questions. We went in 1934, Ada and I. We were 'stretcher cases' but fellows in irons had to sit up all the way, including all night. The atmosphere among the sick is all that the detractors say—intense suggestion. From the religious side, to be one of the pilgrims is wonderful. The full force of Catholic fervour pours round one, and I appreciated that. It was the greatest spiritual experience I've ever had. Since Lourdes I gradually went through it and lost my fervour. I'm sorry. I can't be enthusiastic now.

I can only recall offhand one part of 'The Kingdom' that appeals to me—entry for May 8, from 'The significance of life'; my 'isolation' argument. I suppose it is a happy book, as you say. It could not be repeated. Only now am I beginning to regain some of my former happiness. The 'Tenement' could not appear so happy because I was feeling my way as an individual. Since then I've gained maturity and personal independence at the expense of happiness to some degree.

She made no comment but merely sent him a basket of strawberries with a letter telling how she had been cheated of High Mass, and had to content herself with the second-best, a Low one. Those acquainted with its phraseology will recognize to what extent the despised Penny Catechism has lent distinction to his acknowledgement:

The strawberries were a delight. Jill reaffirms that you are 'a marvellous girl', and like the Law Lords I concurred. That judgement has been given twice. If you disagree you must appeal to the Privy Council or petition the King. I disagree about 'second bests'. It is the idea of the thing that matters. Does your attendance at Mass gain extra glory by being an attendance at a High Mass instead of just a Mass? No Mass can be really 'low'. So let it be with fruiterers, strawberries in particular. After all, the idea is the 'inward grace'. Sacramental strawberries! Now don't go thinking and spoiling that!

Like all the others, this letter opens: 'Dear Mary Tiernan' and is signed 'George Thomas'. Yet by subtle degrees the whole tone of his letters was being transformed. In his Christmas letter of 1939 he dropped her surname and his own. For the next half-year they corresponded once or twice a month. He filled sheets with discussions of style, reminiscences of schooldays, political theory, and musical appreciation, while she constantly urged him to get to work on another book. On June 25 of that year he was caught off his guard for a moment and made a surprising admission:

> I'm sorry about my laxness in writing but I seem to lack the initiative for writing a book—it seems a rather useless thing to do in prevailing circumstances. If I were not naturally a Catholic at heart, few things would seem worthwhile. But if there is one thing that would influence me ultimately to try and write, it is such as yourself.

A thaw had set in. From now on, he began to express something of his innermost self. 'Thank you for a very good letter,' he wrote shortly afterwards. 'There is something that is quite beautiful in some of your letters, a quietness and happiness that satisfies one.' Almost imperceptibly, Mary Tiernan was becoming his sole confidante. As if by some secret alchemy her letters were awakening in him her own spiritual joy. 'If ever letters conveyed happiness,' he wrote to her in May, 'yours have done so; an effortless naturalness that pulses all through.' And again in September: 'Perhaps I have been slow to recognize something always there. Why should you be surprised that I said you gave me happiness in your letters and actions? Surely I must realize something of you from your constancy? Few people can equal your gift to me in your letters.' He certainly needed a friend, for he was losing his supports one by one.

On September 18 he embarked on a long letter in which he set out to teach her the intricacies of musical theory with its mathematics of inversions and diminished and augmented intervals, when he suddenly broke off. Next day he added a hasty postscript: 'I was unable to go on with this yesterday and am sending this on for the time being. There is a spot of bother I must attend to at the moment.' The spot of bother happened to be the housekeeper's formal notice of her intended departure. Since 1937 she had provided for the Thomases' needs at the expense of Mr J.S.L. The latter now decided that he would not replace her. The war had inflicted grave losses upon him and his anxieties were many. During intensive air raids over the City of London, bombs had totally destroyed the greater part of his property in the West End, dividends of some of the share-capital had gone into arrears, and business activities were narrowly curtailed. Moreover during the intervening years, an increasing tension had become evident in the relations between himself and George. Difference of outlook and lack of common ground had led almost inevitably to friction and misunderstanding without assignable fault on either side. On 19 September 1941, as he was in the middle of his letter to Mary Tiernan, George received a letter from Mr J.S.L's personal assistant to inform him that the housekeeper's withdrawal must mark the termination of his benefactions. Two days later Father Napier-Hemy died suddenly from pneumonia. On September 26 George quietly acknowledged J.S.L's communication with a letter that concluded: 'As the housekeeper left, Dan switched on the wireless for some distraction and we found a moment of consolation. We heard, "Glory be to the Father, and to the Son, and to the Holy Ghost", and we all spoke from the same angle—one of faith.' To Mary Tiernan over a month later he wrote: 'You remember the spot of bother that stopped the music lesson? It was Jill leaving. It happened that someone paid her wages and the help has ceased altogether. It was a blow as you can guess, particularly as my father retires next year. On top of this came the news that Father Hemy had died. He had a small fund for our benefit—not much, but a help, and that too looks like failing. So you see, the outlook has not been very bright, which was one reason for my silence.' He then resumed the interrupted music lesson.

All of a sudden, even music became a mere background, a reflection of something both more human and more divine. On November 15, George wrote in answer to her query:

Why are my letters better this year? Well, perhaps we have taken a few further steps along the way. You write because you have something to say, and I notice the gap between my letters to you, which is a good sign of something real and not merely a courtesy correspondence. There is a test you can apply to my letters. I hardly ever use anything to begin with but 'Dear So-and-So'. There are only two people I address as 'My dear'. I recognize this myself and I have a special name for it. I call it my 'intrusive possessive', which indicates to some extent what it means. If the letters in which the new quality is apparent begin with the intrusive possessive, you have the answer. You are a friend of *mine*, not a *friend* of mine.

Only after this declaration did Mary Tiernan make any allusion to her own history. For over three years she had written to him of his work, his difficulties, his future; they had discussed natural beauty, literature and music. He had answered her questions and thanked her for her gifts, but beyond that he had displayed no interest in her as a person. She now informed him why, in her first letter of 1938, she had wanted to analyse the nature and obligations of a religious vocation. Some years before, she had entered a semi-enclosed Order but had been judged unsuited to the life. She had hankered after it for a considerable time after leaving the convent, and now summarized for him what she termed the 'Loss and Gain' of her present activity in the world. Until his death in 1940, she told him, her presence had gladdened her father's last years; she was free to enjoy music and human friendship; and finally on the credit side, 'There is you. Knowing you has brought so much joy into my life that it counts as tremendous Gain.' On the debit side, had she perhaps forfeited greater spiritual advancement? 'It is only in Eternity,' she concluded, 'that that question can be answered.' He acknowledged this avowal on November 22:

I think I have never read anything so frank, so unselfconscious and so direct. I would have thought it ever so painful to count the losses in such things, but you seem to have a credit balance—at least in this world. And I'm sure Eternity can take care of the rest. That knowing me counts as gain in such a context makes me feel very humble and not a little ashamed of myself, for being so stubborn and poor in spiritual things.

With this letter he sent her an autographed copy of *Neighbours* and agreed to listen at the same time as she to a broadcast of Beethoven's Spring Sonata. Eleven days later, he prefaced a twelve-page letter of tiny script with an appreciation of the Sonata. 'It is only lately,' he admitted, 'that I have been able to relax enough to enjoy the special beauty and the emotional message of music—it is like being given back one's hearing and feelings.' Fumblingly he tried to continue and finally abandoned the attempt: 'I've thought so much how I could answer your recent letters but the best way seems to elude me. I thought of quoting some Shakespeare but I doubt if I shall.' For the next six pages he talked of Beethoven, Rachmaninoff, her walk by the river in the rain, her use of Gaelic. As he ambled along, desperately exploring one avenue after another only to land himself each time in a blind alley, the postman delivered a letter from her. He read it, and took a wild plunge:

I wanted you to *say* how the letters pleased you. Your approach was so sensitive that I wanted a more 'real' understanding. I will quote the piece of Shakespeare, or at least the lines that serve the purpose. I want to show you how I appreciate your self-revelations to me. If you know 'The Tempest' you may recall a scene between Ferdinand and Miranda. He finds her one day crying. 'Wherefore weepest thou?' he asks. 'At my unworthiness, that dare not offer what I desire to give,' she replies; and further on, finding courage easy with him, 'Hence bashful cunning, *and prompt me plain and holy innocence.*' (I cannot quote more.) I hope you will see what I mean to convey. I need only add that the part I quote is thought to be the loveliest, purely virginal scene in Shakespeare.

Now there is your point about the 'initiative'. I'm very sorry if your consciousness of it detracted in any way from the pleasure of the journey. This seeming lack of response or initiative in me is not quite what it seems. It is not insensitiveness or conceit or anything masculine like that. Until the time came when you yourself showed in your letters, I could not take any initiative. It is just one of the unhappy things that have come out of my not being a normal able-bodied person. I thought of explaining the effects life has had on my mind and personality, but I feared it might give you pain of sympathy and I cannot hurt you in any way. I must admit that the possibility of the letters ceasing if you did not write was very real. I respond rather than seek. You may have noticed that you had the initiative always. Being disabled, I have never run after friendship. I know when I can open out to a friend, although of recent years I have learned *not* to. I shall tell you frankly where you score with me

above all other women. You are a fine Catholic
and have a good spiritual consciousness, and were
you to be all I could need from one person, I should
still count your spiritual self as one of the best things
in my life.

I have made my own scheme of spiritual things,
but it suffers from the rigours of my life. I am a
rebel who hopes he is on the side of the angels, not a
Catholic resigned to crucifixion with Christ. I
accept that, but make it insignificant by mastering
it—not by asking for its removal. I did not think I
should write all this, but I want to make the point
about initiative seem of minor importance.

When Mary Tiernan received this letter, she did
what any woman would be expected to do—she turned
to 'The Tempest' to place Ferdinand and Miranda in
their setting. And there she read:

FERDINAND: I
  Beyond all limit of what else i' the world
  Do love, prize, honour you.
MIRANDA: I am a fool,
  To weep at what I am glad of.
FERDINAND: Wherefore weep you?
MIRANDA: At mine unworthiness, that dare not offer
  What I desire to give; and much less take,
  What I shall die to want: . . .
                                Hence bashful cunning!
  And prompt me, plain and holy innocence!
  I am your wife, if you will marry me.

She replied by return of post. Almost too casually
she dismissed the subject: 'I took "The Tempest" and

read the passage you quote. Two years ago you gave me a quotation from the same play, "Daffodils, that come before the swallow dares"—but perhaps that is from "A Winter's Tale"?' Then as she dealt with his letter point by point, the joy she could no longer conceal welled up, and she took refuge in Scripture as he had done in Shakespeare:

'Shout with joy to God all the earth: sing a song to his name, give glory to his praise.' It was the spiritual side of 'The Kingdom' that attracted me in the first place. When we began to write to each other, I probably hoped for an outlook in keeping with 'The Kingdom'. You told me you had changed much since writing it, but as our correspondence grew, I found I could talk of the Church with you quite easily, and even discovered that you were not such a rebel after all.

The moment had obviously come when the twists and turns of the zigzag route of their friendship must be abandoned for the perfect frankness that would lead to their manifest goal. But George was still more than half-afraid, unable rather than unwilling to renounce his disbelief. On December 10 he wrote to her:

I don't want you to be a saint yet, but I do want you to rejoice in my joy at your being good. To a Catholic it seems obvious to recognize an outward sign, knowing that a tiny thing can be a gesture towards an inward state even unexpressed. My appreciation of all this is the background to your personality in relation to our human communion, which in its highest form has its own sacrament.

Are men normally stupid? I am thinking that I have been so for a year. I might use your own words 'small and frightened'. I hoped you would find my letter significant. I used Miranda deliberately and hoped you would read it up at once, and if necessary *forgive* me. I wrote 'To me you seem to offer and fulfil at the same moment'. I meant that I heard Miranda, but was afraid!

I think the clearest remark to penetrate my skull was: 'It is not easy for a woman to go into details—the initiative is not her prerogative, and I had to keep this in mind in my reply.' And now I can talk of the *prerogative*. This is where the pain of sympathy comes in. Disablement is one thing; it was my job to cope with it in material and spiritual ways. Socially I was unable to be self-supporting, but I had to learn to surrender human rights. One can manage that, but *not* avoid the consequences. As a result, part of my mind seemed damaged. Were you taught to say at Holy Communion, 'and my soul shall be healed'? I felt the need of that to happen to me. But how? At this point the rebellion began. There are limits to what one is willing to go through without asking questions of life and faith. I would not use faith as a compensation, and to try to be very good might have been self-deception. I found it easier to be a human being and put up with the rest.

Briefly, in affection and in close friendship I found a reservation—'the flowers are not for you to pick'—they were in the garden in which I could not walk, literally because I could not walk. One thing I have known that most normal people never see, and that is that a response from another or from oneself to another is only indestructible and sure if it comes from the life of the spirit. The hope of my soul, therefore, was first the 'spiritual aspect'; if that came to me then I was to give thanks and take good care not to be too sure, say, of a prerogative.

Is that clear? It means that I am very fond of you all the way through. And now forgive me, for I am a poor specimen judged by flesh and blood.

No sooner was the letter out of his hands than his mind once more became a battleground of doubt warring against hope. His sole relief lay in writing to tell her so:

I think you will surely now be hurt by the 'pain of sympathy', but it comes from telling you the truth. The correspondence has grown to the point where the word 'threshold' seems most apt. I am, as it were, holding my breath after having knocked softly on the door. I expect you to answer the knocking, and I shall hear your footfalls as you approach. Since getting your letter I feel I can come quite near and await you at the door, knowing you will respond to the 'initiative' I show! I have at least made use of my prerogative. As you forgive me, my dear, send me a blessing.

I wonder if you have realized it? I think I have been living through and experiencing the *meaning* of the entry for May 8 in both its aspects. It did not occur to me when we were writing that that was happening. The spiritual aspect *first*, and then our mutual confidence. I still wonder at my courage in quoting 'The Tempest', knowing that you would look it up and *wanting* you to do so!

From Dundee she was busy telling him much the same thing at much the same time:

I have found myself thinking of the entry for May 8, of the fact that there are two ways out. Do you think we have found both?

And now 'The Tempest'. When I read your letter the first time, I understood it just as you meant me to. Later—was I reading more into it than was meant? When you said, 'I cannot quote more' I thought you meant you did not know the rest. When I re-read it, I knew at once why you could not continue. Nor could I, for fear I was not understanding correctly; but naturally I wanted to continue the quotation from the point where you left off to the end. Equally naturally I now want you to know that Miranda saw what my own heart said and says. Is that clear?

Do you ever listen to Midnight Mass on Christmas Eve? I should like to make it the centre of our rejoicings. I cannot think of a more perfect communion than this—the central act of our faith. I shall not write during Christmas week. Instead I shall pray for our happiness, a spiritual happiness that nothing earthly should have power to affect, and I shall think of what you wrote on suffering. And when suffering comes, those words which are so true will help us to accept it: 'It seems unreasonable to expect a world to contain happiness that does not also contain sorrow.'

Is this letter of mine quite clear? I hope it is, for it means that my consent is given.

CHAPTER EIGHT · A
WEDDING

1941–1943

She had given her consent, and she had not yet met the man she was to marry. When he broke out into exclamations of wonder at her faith, she returned the rational answer: 'Doesn't it strike you that you have made a pretty big act of faith too? You have never seen me.' And then she blundered. George had concluded his Christmas letter of 1941 by recounting a dream:

> On Monday I went to sleep and dreamed that I knelt at the altar rail for Holy Communion. Behind me was a golden light and a stir of excitement. I've heard that the angels rejoice when a rebel hauls down his flag. This is one reason why I know of the healing. It means so much to me that I cannot follow it with anything of lesser glory, and so, goodnight. God bless us both!

Under the plea of necessity, she dismissed her resolution not to write for a week. 'Do you really mean,' she asked at the end of a long letter, 'that faith has once more become a simple thing? One day, I trust, we shall both kneel together to receive the Bread of Life.' With self-command he quietly discussed the problems she had raised:

About telling the family. I feel strongly that you must not tell them until everything is cleared up and especially until you have seen me. You ask *too* much of them as human beings—a disabled man you have not seen! Not even if I were rich could they easily understand, and I am not even an earner. They might see me as a highwayman: 'Ho, there! Your money and your love!' I cannot say anything until after you've seen us here and know 'the worst'. I hope you are not sorrowing at this moment, but I can't trust my own judgement; I put all this into God's capable hands. I realize that He has given me some realease from my bondage and given me human happiness too. I feel I've been a bad one for being so stubborn a rebel, but perhaps I've had my share and can now grow a little in grace.

This is where my greatest distress must come— how to offset and overcome my disablement. Do you remember this at the end of your letter: 'One day, I trust, we shall kneel together to receive the Bread of Life'? We shall, of course, receive Holy Communion, but I can't kneel. You see how little things to you are the great accumulation of my loss.

With delicacy and precision of touch, she dealt one by one with his difficulties, went into details of her salary, assured him that her use of the word 'kneel' had been merely a thoughtless manner of speaking, and finally spoke of her forthcoming journey to Chilworth:

It is very cold and the snows of January are not far away. Yesterday towards sunset there was a sudden burst of golden cloud in the west, and to the north beyond the scurrying grey clouds, a pink light and blue sky. I thought of the gates of heaven opening. I want our first meeting to take place when April is about to give way to May, almost summer, but with the delicacy of Spring in tree and flower and in men's hearts. This morning, going to Mass, I thought of the visit and was scared stiff. Could I go to Chilworth for a fortnight? No! A week-end? Yes; that would be better. In church my first prayer was for you, and my second: 'Don't let me ever make George unhappy.' That prayer covers every-thing when addressed to the All-Knowing and Almighty. I felt better after that. This week we have the music of Haydn. Shall we be merry too? To be otherwise is profitless when we are entirely in God's hands. He has said, 'Why are ye fearful, ye of *little faith*?' Shall we be of great faith instead?

So they would meet at Eastertide. And then, woman-like, she turned her thoughts to clothes. What colour should she wear? They discussed this important ques-tion from every angle, including that of the necessary coupons, and as she planned the future she forgot her dread, and simply became a girl very much in love.

I'm glad you've lost your fear of the meeting [he wrote to her]. It was not any *use* to you—besides you ought to realize that I shall be here to help you when you come. I don't think I shall even be nervous. I want to be ready to greet you as I have never greeted anyone, so that the years we've been writing will immediately become the years we have already known each other. I am glad that you did not alter Mary for Miranda. You will learn what Mary means when you realize that our Lady's Blue means so much to me—in the sky, for instance. I believe black dresses look well on dark people though I am not an authority. But we are to have blue, so that's settled; it has a message all its own. Between you and the world, like a habit. I call it the apparel of our love. Lately I say my night prayers and have developed a desire to go on praying in-between thoughts until I drop off to sleep. The result is that I am so happy (in the Mozartian theme way) that I don't go to sleep!

Happy he certainly was. An intense joy suffuses the letters of this period. His missal and rosary become as much a part of his life as his love for Mary. With perfect naturalness he tells her that he spent an hour in prayer with her that morning, or else that Lil, his sister-in-law, brought him two cups of tea at midnight since 'praying is a thirsty business'. Lil indeed felt worried at sight of the rosary, George's inseparable bedside companion. 'He's gone all religious,' she complained to Ada. 'Gone?' asked the sister who had known him from birth. 'He always was!' Natural beauty now finds its way into his reflections. In his daily journal, he begins to observe the silver sparkle of ploughed ruts frozen under frost, the dead-white purity of earth blanketed by snow, and the decorative branches and changing hues of trees as they recede on the further side of the valley. But a tiny cloud darkened his sunny horizon. He knew that sooner or later he must inform Ada and Dan of his plans. Commonsense warned him that their reactions might be violent. With a woman's intuition, Lil had already silently noted the steady stream of letters from Dundee and had drawn her own conclusions. When in a vain and clumsy effort to dress unaided, George smilingly remarked, 'I feel I'm making a parcel of myself,' she promptly retorted: 'Then I'll post you to Mary.' 'Do you think she would have me?' 'For about a week,' she replied, 'especially if she has to go out to work.' Needless to say, the two uppermost in George's mind were his fellow-sufferers, Ada and Dan. The nightmare of possible separation had haunted them from childhood. Now that their mother was dead, their lives revolved about George. What would become of them? They had no means of subsistence, their father's pension would not keep a roof over their heads, and they had always looked to their eldest brother to pilot them through troubled waters and steer them clear of debt or public assistance. By some irony, Ada and Dan constantly reverted to the question of what they would do when their father retired and they returned to London after the war. That George might marry seems never to have occurred to either of them. The more he tried to approach the subject, the more he failed, and the more dismal the failure, the more Mary laughed. He got no further than hinting to them that Mary Tiernan was thinking of settling in the South in order to be within reach. It seemed wiser, all things considered, to postpone any announcement of their plans until all had met. So with relief, George settled down again to the congenial task of enjoying present blessings and surveying through half-shut eyes the dreamland yet to be explored:

> I think of you approaching and maybe I shall hear your steps walking to the door. Then hear you speak. And see you, look at you coming into my room. I think of this day as Holy Saturday. Being real to each other is bound to affect us in a special way. Will it mean that everything is enlarged and given the special loveliness we want? Or will it cause you more sorrow meeting me—as I am? You know, you don't really *see* me sitting here, knowing that I am just like *that*, and not as you imagine me. After that comes what, to me, is so lovely in its possibility of knowing the exaltation of being with each other. The mystery of our mutual being. I can't write more of that. I *want* to be silent.

Unlike most, this dream came true. On Easter Eve, 4 April 1942, George Thomas and Mary Tiernan met:

> In the liturgy of the Church, the day was Holy Saturday—an apt and providentially chosen day; not all circumstances are as fortuitous as they may seem. For, in the womb of time, of our time especially, we too had to await the resurrection, the way, and the life, which were to be given to us anew. The resurrection was of hope, the way was of love, and the life was for us both. And the first day was Holy Saturday.
> I think I heard you arrive and knock. I heard Lil go to the door and say, 'Hello, Mary!' as though you

often came like that and this was just another of the visits. Then Lil opened my door a little and you came in, and stood by the books looking at me. My eyes were all for you, but my mind held Lil in the doorway and this tied my tongue. Lil stood for a moment and then moved off—and I was with you, alone and completely aware of you.

I spoke your name. 'Mary.' That was all, and it was at least a minute after you had come into the room. You took my left hand and spoke. 'George,' and you smiled. You were coloured by the air and perhaps an excited nervousness. Your hair was windswept and your eyes alight. You stepped near me and we greeted each other—a handshake! It was a week before I kissed you.

The dominant impression was of being together at last, and belonging. We had opened the book of our life together in person, although at the time it could only be a serial story. You may remember some of the things I said or asked. Did you say, 'You haven't said you love me' then, or was it Sunday? That Saturday we were prepared for our spiritual marriage, but see how Sunday comes in! 'The Dance of the Blessed Spirits' and the music of felicity. You sat in your coat for a long time, and I asked you to take it off. You were wearing a dress of the colour I loved, for me, and for love of me.

After staying two weeks in the village, Mary returned to Dundee. She and George had agreed to marry on July 5, the first day of her summer vacation.

He had at last seen his future wife. So had the family. It only remained to tell them so. During the next few weeks he tried again and again to no purpose. A day-to-day diary kept Mary informed of his mazy progress:

Sunday. I thought to quote the post-Communion for today and so am beginning a letter. 'Grant us, we beseech Thee, almighty God, that we who have obtained from Thee the grace of a new life, may ever glory in Thy gift.' I like the style of this prayer, so like the kind of thing I try to say myself.

There has been a funny side to the past day or so. Ada was with me this morning and I talked of you a lot deliberately, but do you think I could tell her anything? Of course not! No wonder you laugh. I shall talk to Dan first and perhaps that will help me. I wonder what he will say?

Monday. I spoke to Dan last night but we didn't have enough time together. He was a little non-committal then. This morning we continued. He likes you, and that means he can find no reason against you. I said I have to tell him and Ada because we all want to keep together. He has already had a laugh at the thought of Ada, and prophesied her first remarks.

Wednesday. I hoped to see Ada today but she went out. I may be able to talk to her more easily than I thought. It all depends on how much tact I have at the time. Are you still laughing at the idea?

If George Thomas quailed before the prospect of hearing his sister's opinion of his bride-to-be, the first summit conference justified all his forebodings and ended in deadlock. Both Dan and Ada spoke their minds without ambiguity. When they finally reached a full stop, he put in a brief word, firmly refused to give what he called 'defensive explanations', agreed to hold any discussion likely to clear away obscurities, but adjourned it until tempers should have cooled. For a whole month, all three avoided any reference to the question uppermost in mind. At length on May 23 Ada paid George a social call:

After a time, the talk came round to *the* subject [he reported to Mary]. She was very reasonable, realistic, not antagonistic at all, but she sees the difficulties all round. She seemed to take it all for granted, perhaps because she is feminine. She understands why I love you. I haven't said that we *are* going to, but that we *can*. She knows that it is our business and no one else's, and seems to have accepted everything.

From acceptance, she soon rose to practical co-operation. Before long, brother and sister were discussing and scrutinizing the future from every angle to decide how best to act:

A completely happy time with Ada [the next report runs]. I told her of your remark, 'I wish Ada would love me', and she laughed. 'Tell her I don't love anyone,' she said, and added with some subtlety, 'outside of the family.'

While obstacles were being cleared away in one direction, they were piling up in another. Having agreed to marry on July 5, Mary had taken it for granted that she could continue at her post until she secured a transfer to the South; she now learned that her Scottish appointment would be automatically terminated by marriage, and war restrictions made transfer difficult. On July 4 she travelled to Chilworth, but not yet as a bride. Seven weeks later she returned to Dundee as she had come, faced with the distasteful task of baiting officials to explain her private affairs in order to retain her post after marriage. She needed all the moral strength which George's sensitive perception supplied, and when her letters gew heavy with apprehension over the future, he called back yesterday, re-created for her the wonder and beauty of their last meeting, and gently teased her out of her despondency:

We knew in those moments the joy of the other days brought to a point of light that shone in that hour on our love as it was all about us, filling time and the increasing space between us until love itself became an objective thing, an unbreakable link in which separation and distance failed to have any meaning or effect. I shall use that memory as a starting point when I want to be lost with you in a world that can only exist because of its creation by two people who love each other.

It is, of course, a world wherein there are no Corporations or impermanencies. The Authority is the authority of truth, not of standing orders that can be made to sit or take marching orders. Expediency is unheard of there, as is legality, expediency's other self. And Truth is the handmaid of Goodness and Beauty, as the Greeks well knew; those three handmaids whose comeliness of form so entranced Plato.

'They call her frivolous Sal!' Ah, ah, ah (mediant major seventh, sub-mediant minor, supertonic major seventh, dominant major . . .). Ah, ah, ah! And of course I would go and break up a flight of fancy! Just like George—or is it? Few people would accuse him of flights of anything.

'The authority is the authority of truth.' The phrase occurs in a letter of September 27, and is significant. Possibly it betrays the writer's self-conflict. His forthcoming marriage had forced him to face the issue of wholehearted acceptance of the teaching authority of the Catholic Church. To question it had become second nature. He could not deny that he was heart and soul a Catholic, Catholic by birth, Catholic by intuition, Catholic by experience. But that was not enough. Catholic faith demands the whole mind as well as the whole heart, not a fifty-fifty compound of the two. He had already solved the problem raised by St Augustine's use of the word 'memory'. During the previous year, a priest whom he had consulted pointed out that he would find any inaccuracy or obscurity of thought in Augustine's Christianized Plato corrected and clarified in Aquinas's Christianized Aristotle. This sent him to St Thomas's *Summa*. He thus summarizes his findings:

St Augustine's view that ideas are innate and that the divine illumination helps to form them was a combination of Plato and St John on the Word: 'In him was life, and the life was the light of men.' In St Thomas Aquinas I hit upon the very thing that relieved my mind of doubt. He makes knowledge *superior* to will, and so some kind of knowledge has to move the will. Then I realized that memory as described by St Augustine was 'self-conscious'. If it had really known God it would have been conscious of something *outside of itself* as well, and this cannot be assumed.

One out of two difficulties had been solved. He still questioned the Saint's doctrine of original sin. He nowhere specifies his sources and his references are of the vaguest, but apparently what he had imbibed of popular psychology and philosophy led him to formulate a theory in opposition to what he imagined was Catholic teaching. He thus maintained that however much overlaid and encrusted by heredity and acquired habits, 'the real sources of human nature remained uncorrupted', and 'original spiritual integrity' was there in all men to be uncovered and used. He did not stop to define the terms 'real', 'source', or 'human nature'.

In attacking St Augustine's debatable theories concerning the most difficult question in theology, George Thomas could scarcely be expected to propound anything of permanent value where the pens of the most expert theologians have faltered. He was denying statements without any knowledge of the climate of controversy indispensable to any understanding of Augustine's anti-Pelagian polemic. Augustine did not always speak in a satisfying vein, and the Church has never fully accepted his system but has deliberately maintained an indeterminate zone around a problem which on the human level is possibly insoluble. Catholics must believe that by his sin Adam lost the sanctity and justice in which he had been created, forfeited God's friendship, and incurred the penalty of death. But whereas man lost all his supernatural and preternatural gifts, he lost nothing belonging to his nature as man. All the elements, properties, and endowments that constituted his manhood he kept intact and unspoilt, so that the human nature handed on to his children was perfect in its kind. It contained no natural defect or infection or evil inclination which could be regarded as the direct result of Adam's sin. George Thomas had failed to draw an elementary distinction between man's natural and supernatural destiny. His arguments fell foul of the real issue. All the natural virtue in the world cannot fit man for his supernatural end which is, as St John the Evangelist tells us, to see God as He is.

When the Thomases settled in Surrey for the duration of the war, they became spiritually dependent on the Friars Minor at Chilworth. Now there is about a friar, as G. K. Chesterton observed, an element of the tramp or casual labourer. The poverello in his shabby rope-girt tunic, trudging the roads barefoot, was the very sum and substance of George Thomas's social theory and spiritual aspirations, as well as of his personal experience. For St Francis too had known what it was like to eat mildewed crusts. Had he not spread them out on a table of stone beside a sparkling fountain of clear water, and praised God for the vast treasure His providence thus supplied? Thoroughly Franciscan also was the recognition of man's spiritual isolation as of primary importance. 'Carry your cell with you,' St Francis had bidden his first disciples, 'for your cell is your body which goes with you everywhere, and the hermit who occupies it is your own soul.' It was natural that George should be drawn to St Francis' sons. As time went on they paid him frequent visits and he was able to study them at close quarters. 'What I saw,' he says of one of them, 'was a joy and delight. He was still young, a friar, a priest, and a philosopher; and as one might gather from such a combination, a sublime optimist.'

Before long, George was airing his views about the vexed question of the Fall of man and original sin to his friendly listeners. In the middle of a letter to Mary, he breaks off with: 'A priest has come along,' and later resumes:

> He was Father Charles, the Guardian. He is not old, and has a nice face and charming smile. He came to stay a minute which lasted an hour and a half. We had a long chat about the Fall. He explained how Adam was going on a level course as a *natural* man, but possessed also the supernatural gifts which could lead him upwards to meet God face to face. He was given the perfect means but failed, by an act of the will. He agreed that underneath is the fundamental good that I call integrity, and our use of God's grace is the way by which we can regain the chance to see God face to face. This may seem simple to you, but it was not to me.

This discussion was followed up by the loan of books to clarify their terms of reference. 'I read "First Principles of Knowledge" for about thirty pages until I had come up for the third time,' he wrote to Mary. 'It has had one good effect—it is debunking my supposed intelligence. I just can't take in all I read, or even understand some of it!'

The final debunking was the work of an unassuming young friar but recently ordained. Father Anthony had been deputed to take spiritual charge of the three Thomases. It was his custom on the eve of Communion days to drop in and hear their confessions. During the last week of September he made his usual call. George notes: 'Father Anthony went into the other room while I prepared for confession. All I could think of was—well, it doesn't matter. I was surprised at myself in case my memory was bad!' During the chat which followed the confession, George returned to his pet subject, ventilated his views on the Fall, and substituted his own theories as a more satisfactory solution. Father Anthony listened earnestly and courteously. In the past, George had found that priests treated his arguments rather casually. They took it for granted that he was on the side of the angels, enjoyed the little debate, and left it there. Father Anthony reacted differently. Without meeting George's objection, he asked him in serious tones whether he accepted the doctrines of the Church. George had recourse to evasion. The Church's doctrines as a whole did not affect him, he said. He had not made a study of them all, so could not answer with any conviction. The priest hesitated, and in the silence that followed made it perfectly clear he would not at that moment put his penitent to a conclusive test, but would give him time for deliberation. He was due elsewhere and hurried away, to return next day with the Blessed Sacrament.

A few days later, on October 5, he walked in and announced that he had come to salve his conscience. He opened fire at once. 'Do you accept wholeheartedly the *de fide* teachings of the Church?' he asked. George prepared to enjoy a skirmish of wits:

I said I had two things, reverence for God, and humility in the face of Truth. But I could not see any need to ask me to accept all the *de fide* teaching. I don't know it. I always say that any problem decided by an *ex cathedra* statement, unless it is my problem, does not in effect exist for me. As far as the demand to accept the Church's authority goes in all *de fide* statements, the matter concerns not so much truth as the preservation of delegated authority, the power of the Church.

So far, Father Anthony had not had much chance of 'salving his conscience'. But I began on another line. I said I liked talking shop: writing with a writer, music with a musician, religion with a priest, and where I discuss religion, I do so for intellectual purposes rather than spiritual. A quarter to eight and Father Anthony had still to go to Godalming. He spent a few minutes with the others and then left.

George congratulated himself on an easy victory. A week later, Father Anthony paid his routine visit in preparation for the morrow. George was sitting alone. As the priest entered the room, six pips sounded from the wireless, the accepted signal for George and Mary's evening assignation when they both said the Angelus together, he in Chilworth, she in Dundee. George was in a quandary. He solved the matter by asking the priest to say the Angelus with him. Smiling with pleasure, the priest knelt and complied. He then got down to business. Before he heard his confession, he told him, he wished to put to him this question: 'Do you accept without reservation all the *de fide* doctrines of the Catholic Church?' With inward amusement at the resumption of the fight, George adopted his usual strategy. The friar cut him short. 'I should like a plain "Yes" or "No",' he said quietly. All at once the terms 'Church' and 'doctrine' ceased to be abstractions unrelated to practical living. Hitherto George had been in danger of regarding them as things that he could use or set aside at will. Now in the person of a diffident young Franciscan, he was confronted by inflexible authority. This time there could be no evasion and he knew it. To refuse Holy Communion is one thing; to be refused it quite another. There was silence. It was broken at length by George's monosyllabic, 'Yes'. Without further ado, the priest heard the three confessions, stayed to tea, praised the cook for her delicious tomatoes on toast, and said he must be off.

When George said 'Yes', he meant what he said. In that assent he had taken the final leap of faith. The synthesis of his life was complete. He may be left to tell the sequel:

> I realized that I misunderstood far more about Church authority than I had imagined. There is no compulsion. Willing consent is asked. If willing consent is not forthcoming or is withheld or withdrawn through doubts, then the Church leaves

such cases to their consciences and the care of God. Although true conscience will harmonize with the will of God, the Church recognizes that for some reason the conscience may be in error. Naturally where personal convictions become hard and fast through self-will, it is right that faith should be given up. This is the duty of even an erroneous conscience, and it is upheld by the Church.

My new attitude of mind was a clear-cut gain. A real and living Providence came right into the hours, days and years of my imprisonment. Being alive was a new experience, more vivid and significant; to be vague in thought and feeling became unnecessary. Even the sunlight coming into my room had an added warmth, not the soft warmth of its rays alone, but a symbolic almost personal warmth, such as is found in much-loved things and people. There was a blessing in light, and in sunshine the warmth of a new understanding. I appreciated all the more the astonishingly comprehensive statement of St John: 'In him was life, and the life was the light of men.' I found that this light was boundless, not only in personal worship, but in all the ways of life.

The discords of his life had been resolved and he was now a thoroughly happy man. Mary had not yet settled her affairs so their marriage was necessarily postponed. In November George made a playful reference to his health: 'My stomach was a nuisance and a bit painful so I decided to go back to bed. Lil asked if I wanted my usual hot water for supper. I did, having no wish to lead a depraved life intoxicated with tea.' The pain grew worse, and on December 5 he was admitted to the

George Ward of St Thomas's Hospital, transferred in April 1941 from its famous site on the Thames opposite the Houses of Parliament to an Emergency Hospital at Hyde Stile, Godalming. Ten days later, Mary was warned that his life was in danger. She went to him at ance. He was suffering, she was told, from an inoperable malignant neoplastic tumour, and he was unlikely to live beyond Christmas. She said nothing whatever to George except that she was to be allowed to see him daily for three weeks. The ward-sister, 'one of the finest women I shall ever know' George called her, watched her patient in amazement. His pain was such that on his own admission it nearly killed him, and added to all else there was no muscular tone in his whole body. The problem of nursing him defied all the academic rules of the profession, yet he completely ignored his terrible limitations; he never referred to himself or gave the slightest hint of introspection or self-pity. Christmas Day came. He spent the morning singing carols, ate a normal dinner, drank a glass of ale, and at tea sampled the turkey Mary brought. The ward-sister reported that he had remarkable recuperative powers, and the surgeon thereupon decided to risk the knife. George was overjoyed. 'Because I love you,' he told Mary, 'I have no fear of the result.' On January 18 Mr Maybury carried out the surgical operation. Four days later George was sitting up, a new man. 'I report for duty this morning, Sister,' was his cheery greeting to Sister Fricker as she made her morning round. To Mary he remarked happily: 'There are two things that will always mystify science and confuse expert opinion—

the effects of love and religious fervour; just human and supernatural *faith*, whatever the size of the mountains.'

Mary now obtained a three months' leave of absence from Scotland, and when George was discharged from hospital on March 21, she accompanied him back to Guildford. To its two occupants, the ambulance might have been a winged chariot, and the Surrey roads the Elysian fields. When he was able to put pen to paper, George recorded the 'most memorable drive, driving back from the near-dead, driving with love beside me, around me, and right through me, so that I laughed for joy; and, very conscious of the vehicle I was in, I kissed Mary, aglow with her happiness and her gratitude for my preservation and deliverance. She pointed out almond-blossom like a pink cloud just above our heads. The ambulance was the symbol of what I was driving away from, the pain, illness, and fear of death. And driving back to new health, new life, and a new and immense happiness.'

As she was due in Dundee on April 26, Mary at once set to work, completed the necessary preliminaries, and arranged with Father Anthony that he should marry them at 3.30 on the afternoon of Monday, April 12. The most pressing problem now was to get George up the hill to Chilworth Friary. A taxi was out of the question: no one could manage to lift him unassisted. An ambulance was possible but scarcely desirable. There remained an invalid chair and Albert's strong arm. Mary had sounded George's views some months before. 'The wheelchair *does* do something to my mind in these circumstances,' he admitted. 'It reminds me that things are so unequal. The chair attacks my courage. It looks like a symbol of defeat. Yet it is a sign also of something overcome, seeing that I have you and your way of looking upon the chair which has defeated it. "I'll walk beside you" you say. Well Mary, I am humbled by love. And because of you, there is now no special emphasis on your spiritual self; the balance is restored between the spiritual and the physical. I love you both. Completely.'

So a wheelchair it was. In spite of the liturgical season—it was Passiontide and the church was draped in purple—George was in a golden glow of happiness. 'On the twelfth of April, of high and glorious memory,' he notes, 'seven members of the Thomas family attended the Franciscan church on the hill, and eight returned—a Mary being added with the witchery of all the colleens upon her.' A fortnight later, on Easter Eve, she had to leave him to return North. But the glory did not depart from the earth at her going. Nothing would ever rob her husband of his joy.

CHAPTER NINE · READY!

1943–1952

Like Innocent Smith, the hero of G. K. Chesterton's hilarious romance, *Manalive*, George Thomas spent the nine years of his married life perpetually recapturing his bride in order to keep unspoilt the sense of her perpetual value. His journal of 1944 records: 'I see Mary as though for the first time on every occasion. This unchanging freshness is a revelation and a most profound joy to me. I wonder how usual this is with other people?' One day a neighbour, calling at the bungalow, found George sitting alone; she referred sympathetically to his lack of company. That night he wrote in his diary: 'When I see a blue sky, I see Mary blue; and when I look to my heart and mind, I find Mary too. And those who believe that God in His goodness is kind are treated kindly. Not a place here but has its presence, not an object that Mary has not known. I was surprised when Mrs Q. asked, "Don't you ever get lonely?" '

For three months after their marriage, their separation was absolute until in August 1943 Mary received a permanent appointment in London. For the duration of the war however she was obliged to leave George from Monday to Friday. 'A new week of journeyings,' George notes in November, 'and Mary looking as calm and lovely as ever. One of my "beautiful memories"—to borrow in earnest a phrase from the cynics of the B.B.C.—is the image of Mary as she says goodbye: black shining hair, eyes full of life, a rosy untouched complexion that has a glowing beauty that warms my heart, her soft straight look, and the joy of her nature.'

During these years of partial separation, George's life hung suspended between one vacation and the next. He buried himself in Cobbett's *Country Rides* in preparation for their explorations, and as soon as Mary appeared they would set out on their rambles. She learned to handle him as no one else could. Seated in his wheelchair with a few apples and sweets in his pocket, he would go off with her in search of adventure. He found it in the sight of a country road full of puddles, in the patter of soft rain on his face, in resting on a carpet of pine needles in a quiet wood, in halting at the entrance to a winding lane with the question, 'I wonder where this goes to? Let's find out!' It was all wonderfully new to this man of forty. Nature herself seemed to harmonize with his moods, especially at Eastertide. Upon his return home, he would jot down each day's discovery:

Three Lombardy poplars almost yellow in their freshness of leaf. A silver birch clad in filmy green against a background of black firs. Set in the midst of them all a tall cherry tree dressed in snow. The silver birch was lacily dainty in pale green, but the cherry wore a bridal veil and dress of purest white. There was a living quality in the whiteness, an unconscious quiet beauty, but the nearer one approached the more one lost by the intrusion; the whiteness dispersed before one's eyes, as though the beauty unobserved had fled with the approach of human creatures, just as birds may be startled into flight.

There was one journey they made times without number. This was to the Franciscan church on the hill where they had been married. If Mary could recruit help to push George's chair up the slope, they entered the church together; but if no aid was forthcoming, she left him under the shade of a tree and went forward alone to kindle a blaze of light before the Lady Altar, to the delight of the man who saw his childhood's longing fulfilled at last. She always lit twelve candles to commemorate their 'Big Twelfth' (in contrast to the 'little Twelfth' of every month celebrated by George with high holiday), and he would beg her quite needlessly to add a little extra money to her offering, 'for being generous with God,' he told her, 'is the symbol of our desire for greater generosity of heart and mind.'

Marriage did not of course put an automatic stop to all his trials. He still had to bear the burden of his own body. Incidents in his journal speak eloquently of his patient endurance. Once, in an attempt to minimize the hardships her absence involved, Mary dressed George and settled him in his chair before she bade him goodbye. She little foresaw the result:

154

I washed and breakfasted and was in my chair by 7 a.m. It felt like going on night duty. I had all my books and papers near on a chair. During the morning I wrote some letters. At eleven I felt a little sleepy and dozed. At twelve I noticed my arms had gone dead and tried to rise but could not. My arms were caught in the sides of the chair and held tight by my hip bones. I could not raise my head to get any swing that might have freed me. The nerve pains in my hands and forearms increased. By one o'clock I had had enough but no one came. At 1.15 Alfie came and sat me up. I could not let him touch my hands, and I sat for ten minutes or so, grunting mentally at the acute pins and needles.

He made neither complaint nor reproach. In a letter written to Father Kerr, a priest-friend, there is a rare allusion to his own life of prayer which may explain his self-possession:

For years I have been playing a game rather like neutrality in war. Whenever something special comes my way from 'the hand of the Lord', I see to it that I do not take sides, so the provocation fails. All invaders are disarmed, so that I can say: 'The effect of that was quite lost on me, O Lord—so give over!' And I believe He has to a very great extent, for since Mary came I have been only blessed. The final touch of the Lord's hand seemed to threaten life itself, for in hospital they gave no hope. I really think I died then and have actually entered into my reward! Or have I?

The basis of the foregoing bit of fun is that I think we have to abdicate before anything has power over us. We consent to things that burden us, whereas they try mostly to suggest their power to us. There is something too in the idea of submerging in a storm until it rides over.

The man who writes thus had long outgrown the frustrated boy of Berwick Street who would go supperless to bed in order to tame his will into dry submission. 'Since those days,' he explains, 'I have learned a more subtle use of balance. I now accept a difficulty as I hear a discord in music for I know that an instant will come, perhaps as fleeting as the click of a camera shutter, when the change will take place; a quiet and faithful patience is needed for that moment. The last straw is unnecessarily honoured. Our responses are not intelligent by nature, they have to be made so by a wisely relaxed view, and in time trifles seen squarely will return to their normal proportions. "Let not your hearts be troubled" is good advice, not only because of the person who gave it, but because it is a truth of the spirit.'

Never to clear up a situation by force became one of George Thomas's ruling principles. If he applied it to suffering, he applied it still more deliberately to joy. To woo happiness with high expectation of winning and grasping it to the full in this life is to court despair. After his marriage the nature of human happiness became his chief preoccupation. He frequently talked it out with Mary and then set down his conclusions. Meanwhile she was urging him, as she had ever done, to set to work on another book. But, as Father Martindale had once warned him, the imagination needs food. As George lay thinking of the attractive country-side around him, he was both impressed and depressed by the limitations of his own small world. His largest acquaintance, he decided laconically, was with grass, since he had most often gazed downwards to shade his eyes from the glare of light. After twenty-five years indoors, what had he to say? As if to contradict his thought, he was suddenly overwhelmed by the realization of his own happiness. That settled the question. At least he knew himself. He would write a personal book. Early in 1942 he had written to Mary: 'We may be living together when the next book is written—it is very much like the entry into heaven prayed for on the feast of the Holy Family. It is a human heaven that every one seeks.' And now, physically shackled though he was, George Thomas had found his heaven on earth. That perhaps, he thought, was why he could help his fellow men. The workshop in which he had served his apprenticeship had been an uncommonly painful and difficult one, yet he had mastered the craft of living, and believed himself at last qualified to teach others the right use of the tools. He wanted to re-state in his own terms the supreme purpose of human life, and to point out the pitfalls that beset the wayfarer.

The writing of the new book occupied him from 1943 to 1945. He called it *To Dwell with Happiness*, a title drawn from R. L. Stevenson's essay, 'Walking Tours', and he dedicated it 'To St Thomas's Hospital and my constant visitor'—a veiled allusion to his wife, whom he no-where specifies by name. He divided his book into three parts, Life, Faith, Ideas. The first section narrates the external events of his life from childhood to the visit of the Queen-Mother in 1938; the second deals with his own being, and tells of the loss and recovery of his religious faith; the third analyses problems of happiness, morality and law. Much of the first autobiographical section has been embodied pretty well as it stands in this account of George Thomas's life. The work, however, becomes progressively difficult and more abstract.

The axis about which his thought revolves is that incommunicable selfhood called in *My Mind a Kingdom* man's 'spiritual isolation'. Self-recognition—that consciousness of 'I', 'me', and 'mine' which Gerard Manley Hopkins found more distinctive than the taste of ale or alum, or than the smell of walnut leaf or camphor—this specifically human act of self-awareness must, George argues, be made the starting-point if life is to become purposeful. In other words, he wants to introduce an element of contemplation into the fevered activity of today. The main thesis of the book may be summed up in a few lines:

> In our solitary detachment which no human effort can alter, we know that we can look on, and in looking on become aware of what we have to do and be. We have first to recognize the imperishable wonder of being, that we each have one window through which the infinite may be glimpsed, and that by our nature we belong to the infinite. In the beauty and awe of this knowledge we know our personal responsibility and our mystical duty.

He shows himself keenly aware of the attempt made in

this century to wipe out morality and responsibility from the minds of men. All it has succeeded in doing, he argues, is to dehumanize man, to make him the sole freak in a universe subject in every other sphere to the power, majesty and order of the natural law. 'All the lessons of life teach that pain, suffering and moral confusion arise from a neglect of responsibility which in a quiet detachment we know to be a living duty.' But it is not the prevailing fashion to dwell within the clay-shuttered door of one's own soul; men much prefer to wander about in search of novelty and news. The catchwords are space and freedom, and Science is god, salvation and saviour. George saw himself back in Soho, nose glued to the window, making bets with Ada that the innocent prospector below would fall speedy prey to the smooth-tongued, sharp-eyed 'schlapper' to be seen advancing through the throng. In the microcosm of the Berwick Market, George sees the macrocosm of the whole world. There is a Chestertonian ring and brilliance about his analysis of the aberrations of contemporary society:

In these days we are able to marvel only at the wonders of a world of weights and measures devoid of beauty, colour, sound and scent. Nature has been refined out of existence. The final achievement will be to exhibit the structure of the universe in a formula while its mystery remains. The morality today is the morality of the laboratory, of euthanasia, sterilization and artificial insemination as desirable public values; a morality that distinguishes between a machine and a human being solely by the procreative function. Machines wear out and have to be replaced, but man replaces himself.

In relation to primitive man, the wheel is come full circle. Man need no longer stick a pin in an effigy to give pain to a foe afar off, or curse with an incantation. The modern curse is jet-propelled and pain or death is certain. At any distance incendiarism can be sent on the wing. The old gods who roared in thunder and lightning were the servants of man. Our man-gods and magicians are still with us. They wield the new lightning of annihilation. With an atomic flash, they strike, not at a tree, but at the tree of life.

In May 1944 while the book was still in progress, Mary decided to take George for a week's holiday to a spot he was longing to see. She travelled with him in the guard's van, alighted at Waterloo, and wheeled him through the sandbags and rubble of bombed London to Ebury Bridge Road. It is doubtful whether the Cockney's starved roots had ever really thirsted for the soil. Even now George regarded his five years in the country as sheer exile. He admitted that had he stayed in London he would have been a handicap and a nuisance, yet he felt a certain resentment at having missed the fun. Cockney humour, comradeship and courage were the very stuff of life to him, and man was to be found in his fullness on one spot only of the earth's surface—London. It was with deep thankfulness that he wrote in his diary on the evening of May 27: 'Had not been home for five minutes before I knew that I did not want to go back. My armchair felt as big as a bath and I lay back contentedly.' Within a year he was home for good. On 5 May 1945, Mary and he set up house together in their two-roomed flat. 'It was a grand feeling being home at last after six years' exile,' George writes. 'My first permanent homecoming with my wife, so that I repeatedly thought to myself: "Home, home, and life is lovely!"'

Ada and Dan rejoined their father on the same day in the adjacent three-roomed flat. When Mr Thomas retired from work in June 1946, that special Providence of theirs to whom the family always looked came to their aid in the guise of the Welfare State. In 1948, the pension of £3 a week accorded to the completely disabled gave Ada and Dan a measure of independence they had never known. George saw no reason to avail himself of it. Both he and his wife were Franciscan to the core, and were quite content with what they had. In his superannuated leisure, Dad placidly returned to his favourite avocation and turned cook, if only for the restricted and not always appreciative clientèle of his own family. He found innocent fellowship and festivity, as he had always done, over his pint pot at his local club, the Rising Sun. For the rest, he moved round as nimbly as acute rheumatism would allow, passing occasional disjointed and detached comment, a somewhat solitary and enigmatic figure to the end. He departed from life as quietly as he had lived it, on Christmas Day 1953. At his death, with a reasoning that transcended all logic, his children paid him the highest tribute in their power: 'If ever a man was a Catholic, Dad was,' they agreed. Avoiding enquiry, it is enough to record that Mr Thomas was laid to rest beside his wife in Finchley Cemetery with the Catholic rites of burial.

When that came to pass, however, George was no longer there to preside over the family council. But in 1945 on London's VE day, he was very much Manalive, and home and life, as he kept reminding himself, were lovely. As soon, then, as Mary and he had gathered up the threads of their various activities in London once more, George settled down to complete his book. The effort exhausted him but he felt that the idea was good, the aspiration high, and that possibly it was the best thing he had done. With cheerful hopes of success, he had the script delivered by hand to Jonathan Cape's on 9 March 1946. A month later it was returned with a courteous letter wishing him good fortune elsewhere. Of the twelve publishing houses that rejected the book during the next two years, none held out hope of future acceptance. One, Dickens's first publisher, retained it for some months deliberating over accepting it, but with genuine regret the directors finally decided against it.

It is not difficult to appreciate any publisher's hesitation over marketing some hundred pages of undiluted amateur speculation on science, ethics, psychology and morality. A quarter of a century's self-communing within four walls had left its indelible mark. Both subject matter and style are at times bloodless, emaciated, too intense. One longs for the concrete image, the vivid sense-perception. The general reader might flick over the pages with a yawn of incomprehension, the specialist was more likely to dismiss the whole thing as shallow virtuosity. At any rate it was a risk no publisher would take. George came to see that his work lacked balance and was far too abstract. 'It is a hotch-potch,' he sadly admitted, 'and I am a fool.' But he was powerless to remedy it. He was unable to think for long periods together for his disease was making inexorable headway. Impoverished blood deprived his brain of the mental grip and high degree of concentration demanded by really integrated thought.

He was finished with the craft of writing. It was fittingly brought to an end by a grant of £200 from The Royal Literary Fund, made on 16 November 1945. Henceforward human love was to supplant creative activity as the indwelling force of all his days. His marriage marks a break not only in his artistic but also in his social life. With his return to London, life began all over again.

In 1946 he met Helen Thomas, widow of the poet Edward Thomas. They had corresponded as early as 1932 after the publication of *A Tenement in Soho*, when she wrote and sent the two books of her own autobiography. George acknowledged her gift and there the matter seemed to rest. During the Christmas season of 1945 however, after a broadcast talk on her husband's poetry, Helen Thomas made her way to George and Mary's flat. It did not take long to discover that they shared more than their surname in common. The meeting ended in an invitation to Starwell, Helen's home near Chippenham. From this time onward, the two weeks in July or August always reserved for her became the crowning point of the year. 'Memorable, soul-satisfying days,' George called them, 'filled with beauty, friendship, affection and natural loveliness.' Here in the farmhouse set in its four hundred acres, with its flagged pavements, latched doors and raftered ceilings, its eighteenth-century china and carefully chosen books, the three would sit for hours in the glow of a log fire, and talk of Shakespeare and Jane Austen, of Hampstead and Soho, of Robert Frost's befriendment of Edward, and Edward's of his fellow-poet, W. H. Davies. And all the time, Edward Thomas's spirit rested upon the house, and every object in it spoke his name. There were many excursions—to Bath and the Jane Austen country, through the Cheddar Gorge to see the cleft limestone rock at Burrington Combe which inspired the hymn 'Rock of Ages', past old Flemish cottages put up long ago by Dutch weavers, to the village of Biddestone with its grey stone manor house surrounded by farms that seemed, George thought, to have sprouted out of the soil and grown into the landscape. He found the combination of history and beauty an enchantment, and for the first time the Cockney began to falter in his loyalty. By seeing London, had he truly seen as much of life as the world can show? 'An education for the town mind,' his diary notes after the excursion to Biddestone. 'Streets are caverns with the roofs off.' But of the Starwell memories, one was treasured more than all the rest. Helen spent one evening reading aloud four of her husband's poems, and followed them up with his essay, 'At the Cottage'. Soon afterwards she proposed a mystery run. Packing George next to the driver of the car, they set out through Stonehenge, across Salisbury Plain, by way of Winchester and Petersfield to Steep. They drew up before a row of cottages, and Helen showed her two companions the raw material of the poetry she had read to them—'the hoar-green feathery herb' of Old Man or Lad's Love, where it grew in a low thick bush, almost a tree, along with rosemary and lavender beside the door of the cottage in which she and Edward had once lived. The two women then crossed the stile, and while George watched their bobbing figures gradually vanish into the distant foliage, they climbed the hill dedicated to Edward Thomas and made their way to his memorial, a sarsen boulder carved with a quotation from his essay, 'The End of a Day': 'And I rose up, and knew that I was tired, and continued my journey.' Presently they returned to George carrying sprays of blue borage and bryony and, as true pilgrims should, they all finally came to rest before the War Memorial crucifix under the gable set in the wall in Steep village. There before turning homeward they noted his name, prayed for his soul, and gave God thanks for Edward Thomas who laid down his life in 1917 on the Vimy Ridge.

In a letter to Mary, Helen has set down her impression of her guest:

> Here was a man of keen intellect and most sensitive spirit who in one way asked all of life, and in another way nothing. He wanted beauty in all its forms and so read the best writers and listened to the best music, and kept his spirit eager and alert

for any new experience that might come his way. He was one of the happiest people I have ever met for his interest in everything was intense. He had miraculously kept all his mental and spiritual faculties alive and sensitive to the least vibration of beauty, in fun, sympathy or affection. I don't think there was a moment when he was here that his heart was not full to the brim of pure joy. His poor body was inert and helpless, but all the more it seemed his soul could and did soar. Sometimes the look in his eyes—such appreciation, such gratitude, such love—was almost more than I could bear.

Helen was not alone in marking the gratitude which shone out of George's eyes. In some respects he was reduced, as he admitted, to the joy of a child completely dependent on Providence. When he bade Helen Thomas farewell and returned with gifts of eggs, honey or chicken to the grime and ugliness of the City, even the sight of Paddington Station could not tarnish his delight. For Mary was at his side. Throughout the almost delirious pleasure of the Wiltshire interlude, the fact of her presence had stood out like an unchanging ground-bass beneath exquisite interwoven harmonies, imparting depth, proportion and substance to the whole. 'Mary is so attentive, nurse, companion, wife, and altogether a joy,' he wrote at the end of a day full of wonder. 'We are together the whole time and every minute is new, fresh and lively. There was a wisdom in our marriage that confounds the merely worldly-wise. Thank God for her.' Turning to her one day, he remarked: 'I know that if I died, the light of life would go out for you. If you died, the light would go out for me, but I would go on singing my song for what has been, and you would always be in the room with me.' Love had completed its work; it had sweetened, purified, and spiritualized him, and he was no longer afraid to give it expression.

His time was running short. Early in 1951 he was admitted to St Mary Abbots Hospital suffering from jaundice. After nine weeks he returned home past cure to spend another four months in bed. He was determined to go on. His love and courage got him up again, and in spite of recurrent fever he busied himself with plans for the yearly fortnight at Starwell. Dr Carter consented to his going away, since Mary was able to administer the four-hourly injections of streptomycin. To travel by train was out of the question, so on 14 August 1951 Alfie hired a car, supported George with cushions, and with immense care drove him to Wiltshire. George's joy at the reunion needed no words. He had come, and for the last time. Not a word is recorded of the holiday. Two weeks later he said goodbye with that look of gratitude which was to haunt Helen Thomas, and returned to London a desperately sick man. All that can be said of the next seven months is that he remained alive.

On 16 March 1952 he asked for and was given the anointing of the sick and Holy Viaticum. He did not want to die. Thirty-eight years had passed since the over-zealous little eavesdropper at school informed the eleven-year-old boy that the doctor gave him only six months to live. The blue sky on that sunny day had turned to inky darkness, and the hottest sun could not have warmed the small benighted figure who sat on the kerbstone in loneliness and gloom wondering whether there would be sunshine in heaven, and cricket. From that time forward, it might be said of George Thomas that his busy employment pursued with steady and consistent purpose, had been so to live as to be ready to die.

In 1927, his tutor under the N.A.S.U. had set him the following exercise: 'Write a short imaginary dialogue between Commander-in-Chief Cleon and a private soldier Socrates in camp at Amphipolis on "What is life's chief aim?".' The soldier's Greek chlamys covers but does not hide the tattered trousers of George Thomas of Soho:

CLEON: What is the chief aim in life?
SOCRATES: Cleon, my friend, the chief aim in life is the pursuit of wisdom; the wise man pursues not the pleasures of a bodily existence, the very senses of which are continually deceiving us. Wisdom is the knowledge of the real good, and as such is unattainable through the perception of the senses. This life must be spent in preparing the soul for its life with the gods; we must not hold communication with the world around us more than is absolutely necessary.
CLEON: Ha! That is a rich one! Tell me, do you mean that the chief aim in life is the desire for death?
SOCRATES: Laugh not, friend Cleon; that is the truest word you have spoken.

CLEON: Here, then, Socrates, is a sword. Help your-self on towards your life with the gods.

SOCRATES: Jest not. Is it not taught that man is in a kind of prison and that he may not set himself free, because man is the property of the gods?

CLEON: It is.

SOCRATES: Do you believe it?

CLEON: Yes.

SOCRATES: Is it not reasonable to suppose that the gods would punish man for undoing a work of the gods, created by their far-seeing view of what is good for man?

CLEON: Surely.

SOCRATES: Then man must not free himself, but must await the consent of the gods for his death.

CLEON: It is seemingly so.

SOCRATES: May we not consider then that the chief aim of life is that man, unable to free himself for life with the gods, should best give himself to the preparation of his soul for that life with them?

CLEON: It would appear so.

SOCRATES: How then can it best be achieved?

CLEON: Obviously by avoiding all that would prevent the attainment of the desired preparatory con-dition.

SOCRATES: Excellent. What must man avoid?

CLEON: All the so-called pleasures of life.

SOCRATES: Why?

CLEON: Because they obscure true reasoning by making pleasure appear wholly good when in truth it partakes of the nature of evil as well, whereas what is truly good must be *all* good, and cannot be even in the smallest degree evil.

SOCRATES: Better and better. What then is life's true aim?

CLEON: To aspire to attain to the condition of soul that may permit of a life with the gods.

SOCRATES: Wonderful. How then can man best attain to the condition?

CLEON: By preparing for it, and avoiding that which would undo the good achieved.

SOCRATES: Good. Tell me clearly for the last time, what is life's chief aim?

CLEON: The preparation for death.

SOCRATES: Anything else?

CLEON: Yes, the readiness for death.

SOCRATES: So when one has achieved readiness for death, one may feel confident that the claims of the material state are subdued, and that one is fit to live with the gods and the other wise men?

CLEON: Yes.

SOCRATES: Then you have at last achieved wisdom.

In the little churchyard of Upton-St-Leonards in Gloucestershire, there stands a grey stone sun-dial bearing this inscription:

(East)   Man goeth forth to his work.
(South) Children of light.
(West)   The night cometh.
(North) A rest for the people of God.

Rarely has any man gone forth with firmer resolution than George Thomas to the work of 'making the soul like to God', which according to Socrates is his supreme task in this life. That task was now discharged. Night and rest were at hand. He was ready to go.

On 21 March 1952, nine years to the day since he had left it radiant with happiness, he was re-admitted, a dying man, to the George Ward of St Thomas's Hospital, now restored to its familiar site. After a time, blood transfusions gave him a semblance of health, and as soon as he was able, George resumed his daily rosary and added one more symptom to the medical diagnosis: 'I've got a rosy patch on my heart too—love of Mary.' The ninth anniversary of their wedding—the Big Twelfth—was drawing near. He asked Mary to wear a new dress, and himself selected a white Liberty printed silk in preference to her choice of navy blue. At the same time he forbade her to wear her black suit without a touch of colour, 'so that people won't say, "Poor old George!" ' On the eve of their wedding anniversary he insisted on being raised in bed to try to write her a letter, but it was beyond his strength. Next day Mary went to visit him. He could not see the new dress or the letter from herself delivered by post that morning. Sitting at the bedside, she gave him the texture of the stuff to feel, and read aloud her last letter to him. On a small pad of writing paper, she now jotted down the briefest notes of her daily visits to the hospital:

16 April. Sent for me at 8 a.m. to say that George was dying. Father Farmer came and said the prayers. Later George pulled round. Said to me, 'Mary dear, I love you.'

17. Father F. came and blessed him and said all was well with him.

20. He used my name often enough today to make a rosary of Mary's.

22. George himself again. Father Farmer asked him if he would like Holy Communion tomorrow, and G. who has always loved Communion said Yes. I told him I should learn the Slow Movement of the Beethoven Sonata Op. 90 for his homecoming; he hummed the melody and told me to follow the pattern of the music. He held my hand, kissed the ring, and so fell asleep.

23. George a bit tired today. Our time together was lovely and he kissed me goodnight. Sister told me . . . but George still had my smile as if she had told me it was raining.

24. He said, 'Has it been a good time with me today?' I replied that it was always a good time with him. He said he felt he was pulling up.

25. George's mind crystal clear.

26. George's cough troublesome. I did all I could to help by sitting him up and turning him. Once he put his arms as if to box—and I was so delighted that he said: 'So you'd like me to treat you rough?' He also told me that he expected the doctors to do something for him next week. When he was placed comfortably, he asked me to kiss him. I had to wait till nine-thirty so got an extra hour with him—our last earthly hour together.

27. At twenty minutes to nine as I went to Mass, my beloved went to God.

Epilogue

'Every man must die one way or another, and in the final resort is left with whatever he may believe. All through human history these beliefs have not stopped short at the triumph of the last enemy, which to be overcome at all, has to be overcome in advance. Life and death may be enigmas that defy factual knowledge, but at the same time life may yield some of its secrets to the understanding.

'In those long years I had wanted to learn how to live. With the directness of youth I distinguished between learning for the piling up of information, and the useful understanding of the knowledge of life that I acquired. Without being fully aware of the distinction then, I saw that the real power was in myself. We live in two worlds, and the good things of each are different. Poised in isolation, we have to learn the way, the truth, and the life. Everything else must be unlearned if the glory of the inner life is to be rediscovered.

'In setting out to understand how to live, I was slowly led to an understanding of how to die. Jesus taught that self-loss is the way to self-fulfilment, self-abandonment the way to full selfhood; that the way of crucifixion is the way of resurrection. For Christians, this takes the supreme form of directing the love at the centre of self towards God and the will of God, for no other reason than love of the Perfect. Selfhood is then made perfect in transcending self. This was the first law, the great commandment. "Crucified" is the most powerful word in Christian speech. In olden times a man was crucified to death. I have been crucified unto life, and that more abundantly. Deo gratias!'

(From *To Dwell with Happiness*)